PETER GOWLAND'S
NEW
HANDBOOK OF
GLAMOUR PHOTOGRAPHY

Books by Peter and Alice Gowland

How to Photograph Women

Stereo Photography

How to Take Glamour Photos

Glamour Techniques

Photo Secrets

Glamour Camera

Face and Figure

How to Take Better Home Movies

Guide to Electronic Flash

Photo Ideas

Peter Gowland Photographs the Figure

Camera in Hawaii

Camera in Japan

Tender Bough

Famous Figure Photos

Guide to Glamour Photography

Electronic Flash Simplified

Basic Glamour

Secrets of Photographing Women

PETER GOWLAND'S

NEW

HANDBOOK

OF

GLAMOUR

PHOTOGRAPHY

Peter Gowland with Alice Gowland

CROWN PUBLISHERS, INC., NEW YORK

Published by Crown Publishers, Inc., 201 East 50th Street,
New York, New York 10022

CROWN is a trademark of Crown Publishers, Inc.

Manufactured in the United States of America

Library of Congress Cataloging-in-Publication Data

Gowland, Peter.
   [New handbook of glamour photography]
   Peter Gowland's new handbook of glamour photography / by Peter
Gowland with Alice Gowland.
      p.   cm.
   1. Glamour photography.   2. Photography of women.   I. Gowland, Alice.   II. Title.   III. Title: New handbook of glamour photography.
TR678.G683 1988
778.9′24—dc19   87-33214
                                                         CIP

ISBN 0-517-56898-5

10 9 8 7 6 5 4 3 2

CONTENTS

INTRODUCTION

Looking back on our careers in photography, I realize that, quite un-intentionally, Peter and I have spent a large part of our lives teaching others about the field of glamour. Over eighteen books, hundreds of articles, and over one hundred lectures or seminars have been a continuing learning process for us.

So, here, with our twenty-first book, what *new* can we say? Well, there really isn't anything original in this world—there is only rediscovery or a new approach to something old.

If there is a thread running through Peter's philosophy, it is that photography is basically the understanding of light. Photography is many other things too: composition, framing, selecting a subject, but at the core is perception of light as it strikes the subject. Peter is on a continual search for a simple formula to explain this seemingly confusing element of a photograph.

In our last book we used diagrams to show placement of lights. Here, we've gone a step further and ask that you think of the direction from which a light comes in terms of a number. That was Peter's idea and at first I balked, thinking it was silly, but once I tried the system, I found that I *do* have a better understanding of what effect lights have on the subject whether the subject is a person, a building, or an animal. I'm pleased with myself when I can look at a picture and call out that it is a 1-4-4 or a 2-2-5.

Concurrent with this, we illustrate the type of shadows these various number placements create, and we hope that by studying them you will learn what is flattering and what is not. It takes a bit of practice. The majority of new camera buffs cannot "see" shadows. They may look at a picture and know they don't like it but haven't the faintest clue why. So, we're hoping you'll make a game of this by studying the photographs in this book and in other sources and that you will be able to call out the placement of lights by their numbers and will recognize the benefits and drawbacks to the subject. In the end you'll find it all boils down to *simplicity*. More lights do not necessarily make a better picture. You may find this statement a bit contradictory when reading about effects in chapter 10, but on closer inspection you'll see that even though five lights may have been used, the key ones, those that decide whether or not the lighting will be flattering to the model, come down to one or two. And, most important, their placement—usually a #1 or #2 position.

Simplicity is another thread that runs through Peter's photographic techniques. Often, we carry out complex assignments with a crew of two—Peter and I. Contacting the model or agency, getting the costumes, props, supervising the model's hair and makeup are all part of my job. Peter sets up the lights and background, loads the film and cameras, makes sure everything is in working order. If something needs to be constructed quickly, like a box or a ramp to lean on, he can do that too. When the actual shooting takes place we take turns making suggestions as to the model's pose. If we don't agree, we shoot both ways. We may end up switching jobs: I find myself loading film, he's advising the model about her makeup or hair. We're both Aries so have pretty strong opinions but, amazingly, have managed to survive through this compromise system.

Long ago we decided that we did not want to be involved with a huge studio and dozens of employees and the general public. We prefer to keep control by having only the two of us as bosses. And we like working for corporations rather than photographing private individuals, who sometimes have trouble paying their bills—and who also try to tell us how to take their picture! Even so, we do some complicated commercial jobs, using an 8 x 10 camera and with an art director or client to supervise. In these cases we hire a makeup artist or home economist (when food is involved). Our 20-by-20-foot studio is large enough to handle a kitchen setting made up from a combination of Peter's imagination and parts of my stove. In the finished picture it looks perfectly real. But we always aim for the smallest crew possible.

Don't be discouraged about finding models. Even here in Hollywood we can't find as many as we need. One of the reasons is our selective approach. All young girls are pretty with their fresh complexions, firm bodies, and enthusiasm for life, but knowing which ones will be the easiest to photograph takes an experienced eye. Remember, everyone has at least one good angle, but in our work, where we hope to sell pictures as calendars or posters, we need a model who looks good at *any* angle. We recommend that those of you who hope to make a career of glamour photography be selective in whom you choose to photograph.

On the other hand, if this is just a hobby, then work with those "almost-made-it" young women and you'll be surprised at how happy you'll make them and yourself if you look for the best facial and figure pose and lighting.

Throughout our lecture tours we've found that husband-and-wife teams are popular in the field of photography. Today many work together in the new "boudoir" photography craze. Usually the wife handles the bookkeeping, appointments, and so forth, and the husband takes care of the technical details. Both of them work at the creative end. The idea of having a studio in the home is also growing. We've done that from the beginning and what it amounts to is that you either feel you aren't really "working" or that you're working too much! However, our consensus is that we would not have it any other way.

Photography is still fun and exciting to both of us and we hope that by reading the bits of advice taken from our personal experiences you will find the same joy and pleasure in the glamour field.

UNDERSTANDING LIGHTING

When you think of lighting, try to forget if it is sun, incandescent, electronic flash, or even candlelight. Instead, consider the direction from which the light hits the subject and how many different sources are involved. The subject could be a person, a building, a scenic. Once you have trained your eye to "see" how light affects the world, you will make better choices as to time of day (when using sunlight), placement (when using supplemental lighting), and the number of light sources you want to work with. You will be able to look at a picture and tell by the shadows from which direction the light is coming. The catch-light in the eyes will reveal how many lights were used and the size of the lights. It can become a game, and every time you test yourself, your knowledge of lighting will become more intrinsic.

Every picture in this book will have a formula number so that you can duplicate the same effect for yourself. At first you may have to refer to this chapter to see how the numbers apply to the placement of light. Soon you will know just by the numbers and not have to refer to the diagram on page 3. In the future, any picture you look at will trigger a set of numbers or even a single number. You might say to yourself, when looking at a photograph, "That is a 1-4-4," and know immediately where each light was placed.

In the field of glamour there are light placements that consistently yield the best possible results. I think of them as formulas. You may depart from these tried-and-true systems, but before you break the rules, you should know just what these formulas are. A popular example of an artist who successfully broke the rules is Picasso, but he succeeded only because he learned the basics first.

Using the Basic Lighting Positions diagram as a guide, read the following explanation of how each light direction affects the subject.

FRONT LIGHTING (#1)

The light comes from the direction of the camera, as close to the lens as possible. In glamour portraits this placement is the most popular. If you could set the light in front of the lens the lighting would be perfect—flat. That is what you are trying to do—wash out any shadows on the face, make wrinkles disappear. But, since you cannot put the light directly in front of the lens, you surround the lens with light instead. My personal preference is to use translucents on each side of the lens. Another method is to use three big lights around the lens: one above the camera and one on either side. Or, you could use a single large, soft light above the camera, as close to the lens as possible and then place a highly reflective mirror, piece of Mylar, or silver Reflectasol between the camera and the subject, low and just out of camera frame. The point is that with this method you are getting as much light as possible on the model's face from that important direction, #1, the *front*.

Remember, we are not talking about "character" portraits, where lines on the face are important. We are speaking solely of glamour.

THREE-QUARTER LIGHTING, FRONT (#2)

A single light strikes the subject from a 45-degree angle and can come from either right or left of the camera. For full-lengths I find that the models can tolerate a three-quarter light because the face is such a small part of the total picture and the body becomes the most important aspect. The figure needs a three-quarter light to bring out the shape through the use of shadows. I use this for torso and full-length glamour, both indoors and out. Three-quarter front lighting is perhaps the most popular in the history of art. When you study the masters, you learn that they used what was available to them: a large window light from the three-quarter side.

SIDE-LIGHTING (#3)

Again, the light can come from either side. Usually side-lighting is for dramatic effect where the artist/photographer wants to illuminate one

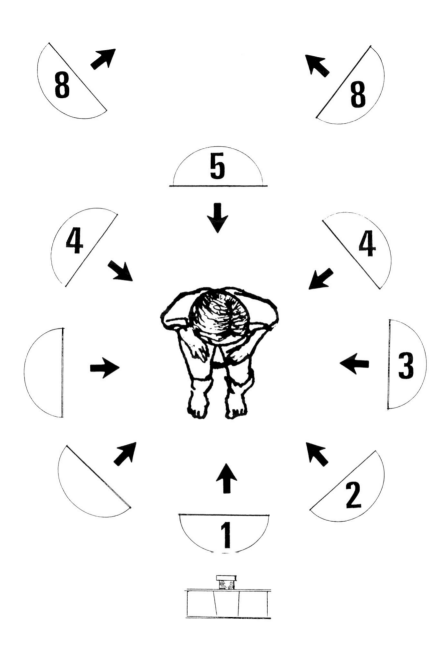

BASIC LIGHTING POSITIONS

side of the subject and throw the other into shadow. We see this technique used in movies, TV commercials, dramatic situations. I find it useful for photographing the nude body when I want to suggest nudity and yet not show every detail—half clothing the body with shadows.

Without another light from the front to fill in the hard shadows of side-lighting this direction can be very harsh for portraits. Some photographers have referred to it as "hatchet" lighting. But the effect can be dramatically pleasing if it is modified.

One means of softening the intensity of the shadow area is by using a second light from the front. It might be half as strong or a quarter as strong, depending on how dramatic an effect is desired. Diffusion with gauze or a glass filter over the camera lens is another method. For variety the model can face the direction of the light, with the front of her face illuminated and flattered, while the body remains dramatically darker.

Sometimes, with side-lighting, I depend on the skill of a retoucher to soften any lines on the face. However, a 2¼ x 2¼ negative is the absolute minimum size to work with. Naturally, 4 x 5, 5 x 7, or 8 x 10 is even better. One of Hollywood's most famous movie portrait photographers is George Hurrell. I had heard that his retouchers worked eight hours on a single 8 x 10 black-and-white negative. When I asked him about this he said it was more like sixteen hours! His portraits of the stars are still popular today and many newcomers to the field are emulating his style. He is known for the use of extremely "hard" lighting. Just about every picture is the #2 (three-quarter) or #3 (side-lighting) direction. He never used a large, soft source such as an umbrella or a large translucent screen to widen and soften the light. Small, hard spots were his favorite. But it takes a dedicated master and a good retoucher to use this most unflattering light source. The effect, as proven by his popularity, was always sensational.

THREE-QUARTER BACKLIGHTING (#4)

The light comes from a 45-degree angle *behind* the subject. Again it can be from the right or left of the model. In fact, one can use two #4s—one coming from either side. This would be referred to as a Double 4. Number 4 lighting is rarely used as the main source. The applications I can think of are with the nude body and when dramatic profile portraits are desired. Clothing the figure with shadows is a favorite technique of mine. There is no better way to do this than with the placement of one or two lights in the three-quarter (#4) rear position. The front of the subject is completely black, almost a silhouette, with the edges of the body receiving varying degrees of illumination from very dark to light.

The following four pictures were made with the key light in the #1 position (next to camera).

This picture was taken with a Larson 72-inch Swing Light behind the camera in front position and slightly above. The large size of the reflector produces such a wide source of illumination that it is like having lights on both sides of the camera. A person learning to understand lighting should look for the catchlights in the eyes, which will indicate the size of the light as well as how many were used and from what direction. Only two additional lights were used here: one above the model to light her hair and one on the background. These were small electronic flash units, used directly and not bounced, as was the key light. Hasselblad with 150mm lens; negative slightly retouched. *Model, Stephanie Drake.*

Four 36-inch Larson translucent square umbrellas surround the lens, two on either side. (Note catch-lights in model's eyes.) Four Larson Strobosol electronic flash units were fired through the translucents, giving almost the same amount of area of diffusion as the one 72-inch umbrella but with weaker shadows. This is the most flattering kind of light for portraits where one wants to wash out imperfections such as wrinkles. Model Shelly Winnaman, of course, did not need that. Hair is lit partially by window and by hair light. Hasselblad with 150mm lens; slight retouching on 2¼ negative.

Technical details here were the same as for the picture on page 5 but one of the four lights (camera left) was turned off in order to create slight shadows. Count catch-lights in eyes. *Model, Shelly Winnaman.*

An aluminum box built around the camera, and containing one tube, just above the lens, creates this "ring" light picture—shadowless. Note lack of texture in bricks and lace. The tube used in the ring light was an 800-watt-second Norman electronic flash. Hasselblad with 80mm lens. *Model, Amie Johnson.*

Now, turn the three-quarter backlights away from the subject and onto the background with a small quantity of the rays still hitting the subject. The white background acts like a reflector, bouncing back a small amount of light. This lighting is extremely delicate because the body is almost completely in shadow, with a touch of spill on the edges.

I use this Double 4 lighting both indoors and out. In my studio, I combine it with the #1 light. Usually the model is against a dark background. The Double 4 hitting her from three-quarter rear makes her stand out from the blackness, and the #1 lights the front of her.

Outdoors, I use the sun as a Single 4 with a #1 (front light), a strobe, which is placed close to the camera. The sun, strobe, and reflectors are merely *sources* of light that the photographer can bring together in a symphony of energy to enhance his subject. Because the strobe illuminates only during a short exposure, when it fires the model's expression is relaxed and not squinting.

Since the sun is a hard point source that casts shadows, I move it behind the model into the three-quarter position. Yes, I said I move the sun. I prefer to state it that way to prove the point that the photographer does have control of light. There are times when the cluttered background makes it difficult to accomplish this because placing the model with the sun in the three-quarter position may put her in front of distracting buildings, trees, or lampposts, so a little added searching for the right spot is necessary.

It is possible to use the sun as a Double 4 light source by placing a large, bright reflector opposite, catching the rays of sun on its surface and reflecting them back onto the model. This is a type of triangle lighting. I call it my 1-4-4: one light from the front and two from three-quarter back (the sun and a reflector).

The same result can be achieved by using a second strobe in lieu of a reflector. I put it on an extension with a photo-eye on the strobe that picks up when the main source is flashed.

Another Double 4 situation might be under trees where you have no sunlight available for backlighting. Here, you can use a strobe from either side and a third on the camera. Anyone viewing the photo will think the backlighting is the sun.

When using a strobe in conjunction with the sun the trick is to keep the light in balance and not have the strobe overpowering or too weak. Both of these situations will result in a "phony" look to the picture.

To recap, remember that three-quarter backlighting (#4) is good for edge-lighted nudes, dramatic portraits, and silhouettes and in conjunction with front lights as an impact to separate model from background.

The following three pictures were made with the key light in the #2 position.

The Larson 72-inch Hex on the Gowland Swing Light system is placed at the #2 position camera left. Model Shari Lynn's head is turned toward the light for the most flattering result but her body is flat on so that the light hits it from a 3/4 angle, thus accentuating curves and cleavage. One hair light from above and four lights on the background were used to give a poster effect. Hasselblad with 80mm lens.

Using a black background and placing key light in the #2 position (3/4 from camera right) adds shadows to model Lisa Greer's face and body. Four backlights (at #4 position), two from either side, edge-light the body and head and separate her from the dark background.

Here, the sun is the only source of light. It comes from the #2 position camera left. Since not many models can look into the bright sun, it's quite believable to have the eyes closed for this relaxing beach scene. Hasselblad with 80mm lens. *Model, Georgette Welborn.*

The following nine pictures were taken with the key light in the #3 position (90-degree angle to the model).

Even the most beautiful models are at a disadvantage with this harsh side-light—unless retouching is done on the negative. Many photographers call this "hatchet" lighting. The right eye is barely visible. Two additional lights were placed in the #4 position, one at either side, hitting her hair and body from both sides. Without the use of these #4 lights, the model would have disappeared into the background. This lighting can be modified with a smaller front fill light from the #1 position (front, next to camera). *Model, Karen Witter.*

Texture is emphasized by placing the light at this 90-degree angle. Both the lace and the bricks now stand out and shadows appear on the wall. This lighting tends to add drama to pictures and is excellent for character studies. Only one light was used—the Larson 72-inch Super Silver Hex. Hasselblad with 80mm lens. *Model, Amie Johnson.*

BACKLIGHTING (#5)

The light source comes from behind the subject. It can be placed behind the head so that rays come through the hair or it can be raised slightly so that it lights the hair from above. In this position it is not a top light because it is still behind. Like the #4, it edge-lights the head.

Care should be taken that when the backlight is in the raised position it does not strike the camera lens. Sometimes a good lens shade will work, but a better method of preventing this "flare" on the film is to have a screen, placed on a stand or taped to the light, blocking the light from hitting the lens but allowing it to hit the model's head. This is called a *go-bo*. I think the term comes from the words "go between." A third way of keeping the backlight from hitting the lens is to have a *snoot* on the light itself. A snoot is usually a metal tube that contains the light, aiming it toward the desired direction, like a pipe directs water.

In most cases, backlighting is used in conjunction with other lights. A favorite portrait technique of mine is to use a #1 (front light) with a #5 (backlight). The front light is usually a Larson Soff Box, placed directly over the camera and as close to the lens as possible. As I mentioned earlier, a bright reflector is placed between the model and the camera, out of frame. This can be on a stand in the flat position (like a table) or placed on a table. The model can lean on the table with elbows resting on the reflected surface. It is just out of range of the picture. This reflector is doing the work of a third light. The effect is great; it picks up the light from the Soff Box and bounces it into the model's eyes and under her chin. If she happens to be smiling, her teeth are lighted beautifully.

The backlight (#5) is behind the head, outlining the hair against a black background. I like this setup because it is infallible and requires the absolute minimum of equipment.

The photographer without a studio has only two lights and a cloth background wherever he goes. Even a light background with no illumination on it will turn dark if the model is posed some distance from it, whether it is a wall, curtain, or foliage.

Now you have my five directions of light: front (#1), three-quarter front (#2), side (#3), three-quarter back (#4), and back (#5). When you look at a picture in a magazine, on the movie screen, or on TV, you will start to see from which direction the light originates. In most cases glamour magazine covers are using front (#1). Most movie close-ups and medium shots are three-quarter front (#2). Night shots on movie screens are usually blue side-light (#3) to give the feeling of dramatic night. Very dramatic mood shots are three-quarter backlight (#4). Almost every scene in a motion picture uses backlight (#5). This is especially true of the classic movies, where lighting was more pro-nounced. Today's moviemakers go for the more natural lighting even if it is unflattering to the actors and actresses.

As complex as lighting may seem at first, it becomes simple when analyzed. Find the main light (generally called the "key") and you will have the formula. All other lights in the picture are supplemental—they are used to accent or to modify. Remember also that the most respected artists and photographers keep their lighting simple—the impact comes from dramatic shadows. When an artist selects a particular lighting he is deciding where the shadows should be. He depends on the angle of light to give roundness to his subjects, a roundness that is evident from the dark edges of the figure or face. It can also be termed "third dimension." The degree depends on how far around the key light is moved. But, remember, you face a trade-off here. While this edge may give a third dimension, it also can be cruel to bodies and faces with imperfections, lines, wrinkles, or excess flesh. If it is character you want you needn't worry—use the #2 or even the #3—but if glamour is your aim, keep the light (#1) as close to the camera as possible.

There are three other types of light placement, which are not included in the diagram (page 3) because they are used sparingly, but I will discuss them just so everything is covered.

BOTTOM LIGHTING (#6)

The #6 comes from the direction *below* the chin, from the floor or ground. It is the most unflattering light possible for people. Horror movies employ this to give a sinister look to villains. One particular application that I have used it for is in the campfire situation: a romantic setting outdoors where a couple is looking into the flames. To get a realistic effect the bottom lighting (#6) must be used. I have placed logs in the foreground and used an extension strobe behind the logs, pointed toward the couple. The logs hide the strobe from the camera. The sun is behind the couple, and I must shield my lens from its rays with a go-bo held by my assistant. I have also placed a yellow gel over the lamp head of the strobe to give the light warmth. By having the models look down, directly into the light, it almost becomes a (#1) front light and thus is not unflattering. If the subjects were looking into the camera, instead of down into the firelight, then the shadows would be unflattering. To make the picture even more realistic, I do not develop the transparency immediately but use my fireplace to add flames to the bottom of the picture by means of a second exposure on the same piece of film—the result, realism.

The dramatic side-lighting is excellent in nude studies because it gives definition to the body. By turning model Sara Munson's head slightly toward the light we can see her right eye, which would be lost otherwise. One 72-inch Hex came from Sara's left and the background light came from the right so that she had a dark background on the light side of her body and a light background on the dark side.

Full-length with same lighting setup. *Model, Sara Munson.*

Same lighting but here the background is lit from both sides and the model rests on Mylar. Hasselblad with 80mm lens.

TOP LIGHTING (#7)

In most cases I avoid this direction of light. It comes from above, shooting directly down. The sun at midday, for example, is top light. For some reason, and I suspect it is laziness, TV newsmen use this unflattering #7 for most of their personal interviews. All that is seen on the screen is the shape of a face with black sockets for eyes and a cone for a nose. I have used this type of lighting only in one particular situation: when we were working at the beach early and have extended into the noon hour. The model can assume a horizontal pose, as though tanning, turn her face upward, directly into the sun, close her eyes, and the picture will have a natural look, good as a stock photograph for sun-tanning lotions or health-minded products.

In motion pictures this top light is used for effect. In the film *The Godfather* top lighting was used for most of the picture. Inside sets were scantily lit and only from the top of the room. The result was a heavy, dark, and moody setting where the viewer sometimes had difficulty in making out features or faces—exactly what the director wanted. It certainly has no place in the bulk of glamour work, but I would not eliminate it completely in areas where a photographer is conducting experiments in creative imagination.

I have noticed that many of the clothing catalogs do not mind using this top light. There are probably several reasons—one being that when photographing clothing, one must work fast, a lot of changes in one day. It is quicker to use the available light than bother with strobes or reflectors. Also, the clothing is the star; models' facial expressions are secondary and are usually not playing to the camera, so in this area sunlight, even at noon, can be used.

SILHOUETTE LIGHTING (#8)

Number 8 lighting refers to light that does not hit the subject. It is directed away, onto the background. Some of my favorite figure studies have been made with this type of lighting. Sometimes I use as many as four lights, directed on the wall of my studio. But, in lieu of a studio, a window will suffice. Using strobes against a white, curved wall, with a figure posed or dancing in front of it, allows a small amount of the light to bounce back, thus giving a vague sense of detail to the body, rather than an inky black silhouette.

A reflector, placed at a 90-degree position to the right, picks up the sun, which is in a 45-degree rear #4 position. This type of harsh side-lighting is excellent for nude studies. Note that foliage in the background is receiving no direct sun and only small amounts of backlight filtering through the leaves, creating an interesting pattern. Hasselblad with 80mm lens. *Model, Heather Haines.*

At sunset the sun becomes a low #3 light in this pose of model Suzanne Copeland. No additional fill light was used.

The wet sand turns black when the sun is in a low 90-degree #3 position. One has only a few minutes to work in this kind of light because the sun is disappearing rapidly. Hasselblad with 80mm lens. *Model, Suzanne Copeland.*

Sunlight late in the day, in the #3 position, casts long shadows of model reclining. Hasselblad with 80mm lens. *Model, Shelly Winnaman.*

The following three pictures were made with the sun in a #4 position, 45 degrees from the back.

Window light only. If model had not turned her face toward the light, there would have been no light on it at all. No additional lights used. *Model, Shelly Winnaman.*

Here, the daylight comes through a window at a 45-degree right position and from a door (not visible) 45 degrees left. This is my favorite lighting for nudes—keeping the body half in shadow. Setting was a barn. Pentax with 50mm lens. *Model, Shawna Roebuck.*

Late afternoon sun in the #4 position makes a nice silhouette of a nude walking in the surf. Hasselblad with 80mm lens. *Model, Denise Oldenberg.*

Additional photographs with light in the #3 position.

Model walks in shallow surf; sun is in the #3 position, low in the sky. Notice the change in shadows on the body as she turns slightly more toward the sun. Since the sun is so low on the horizon there is very little reflection from the surf, causing the shadows on her body to be darker than usual. Hasselblad with 80mm lens. *Model, Denise Oldenberg.*

I have discussed eight types of light directions. You will, in most cases, be concerned with using #1, #2, and #3. All other numbers are supplemental. Your model's features will determine which lighting is best. Here is where your ability in selecting the most pleasing shadows or lack of shadows will be tested.

In my studio I have a mirror on wheels. On occasion I play a game with my model. I seat her in front of the mirror, then move my 72-inch Larson Super Silver Hex with modeling light into different positions— #1, 2, and so on. I ask her to tell me when the light is most flattering. Invariably she will pick #1.

An example of lighting that comes from all sides: a bright day with the sun overhead lighting the foam, making it a giant reflector. Hasselblad with 80mm lens. *Model, Georgette Welborn.*

No additional light was needed for this picture taken in an all-white room with windows on all sides. This proves an exception to the rule that says one can see the direction of the light in a photograph—here, the illumination comes from all over. Hasselblad with 80mm lens. *Model, Debra Gaske.*

These three pictures illustrate how shadows on the body change with the placement of the key light. For example, the first picture was taken with two lights in the #1 position, one on either side of the camera. In the second picture, the light has been moved to a #3 position, above the model. In the third picture, the light is in a #4 position camera left, at a 45-degree angle from the back. These were all taken in the same location but look different because the background was overexposed. Hasselblad with 80mm lens. *Model, Yvonne Thomas.*

Above: Model Yvonne Thomas stands at a window with daylight, the only light source here, coming in through the lace curtains in the #5 position, from behind the curtain. Hasselblad with 80mm lens and Verichrome pan film.

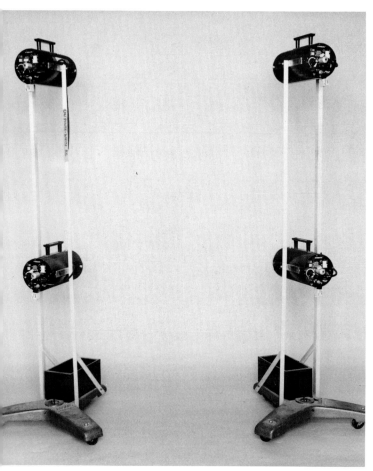

Three uses of the Larson Strobosol lights

I made these stands for my Strobosol lights by using two cast-iron Ascor bases (vintage 1955) that I had on hand. The supports are of 1-inch aluminum angle. One light is 28 inches from the floor and the other is 62 inches. This latter elevation works out well for a full-length picture because it lights the background evenly. Wires run down the base, which is connected to the wall. Each Strobosol has an electric photo-eye that picks up and fires simultaneously with the key light. Each lamp has a pilot light on a dimmer and an adjustment for the amount of power of the electronic flash. On white backgrounds these are turned down to half-power. Shields are used to prevent the lights from hitting the model. The two boxes on the base of the stand are used to store the electrical cord.

When the Strobosols are used as backlighting (#4 position), four aluminum reflectors are attached to the four heads. This concentrates the lights in a certain direction and keeps them from hitting the background. Shields are placed between the lights and the camera to protect the lens from being hit.

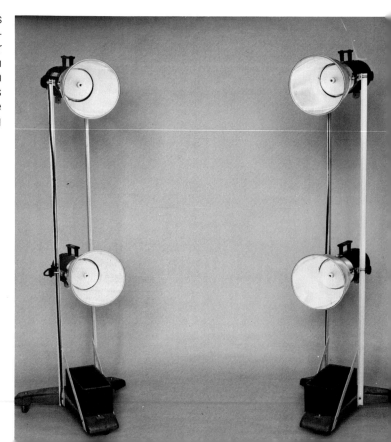

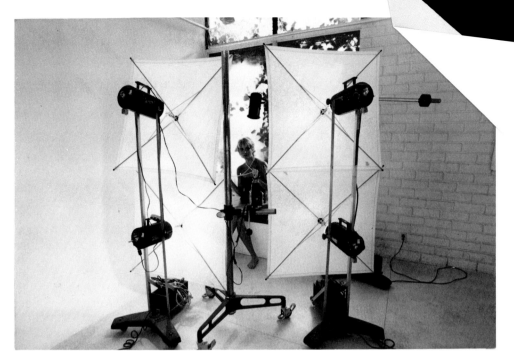

Using the Strobosols to create a bank of light 6 by 6 feet (I call it my "wall of light"), I insert the stem of a 36-by-36-inch Larson translucent into the hole in the front of the lamp, which continues through the middle and is tightened on the other end. The camera is set up between these two stands, and thus the subject is surrounded by the softest, most flattering light. These can be used separately to light the model full-length when you want to have some shadows on the body.

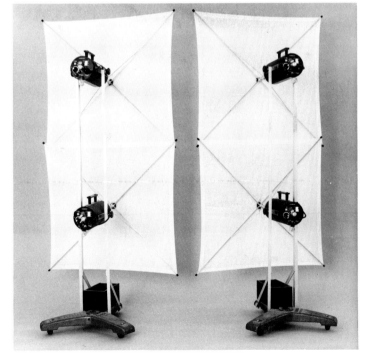

My Hasselblad with an 80mm lens (Zeiss Planar f/2.8) is probably my most often used equipment. I prefer to shoot most of my black and whites on 2¼ x 2¼, and the Hasselblad is my favorite camera for this format. The Norman 200-B is on the camera in the #1 position with the sun coming in at a #4 left. *Model, Stacy Alden.*

2

CAMERAS, FILM, PROCESSING, AND FILING

I began to take up photography seriously when I was in my late teens and in looking back credit my job as an extra and sometime bit player in the movies for creating that interest. That environment also influenced me toward glamour. The long hours of waiting around on the sets would have been intolerably boring had I not been intrigued by two things: the work of the lighting crew as directed by the cinematographer in placing the giant, incandescent lights, and the pretty girls, always in abundance.

There were several others who found these subjects more interesting than watching the leading actors and eventually we formed a camera club and called ourselves the "Hollywood Camera Clique," a fancy name for an unsophisticated bunch of hams.

CAMERAS

Then, as now, we all had the same naive wish: to own a camera that could do everything! My friend and fellow actor Carlyle Blackwell chose a rangefinder Leica and I was sold on the Rolleiflex. From the beginning I preferred the quality of the large negative and Carlyle liked the advantage of faster lenses and the ability to use a variety of focal lengths on one camera.

Today, the same question of which camera to purchase is an inescapable dilemma to those interested in pursuing glamour photography either as a career or as a hobby. In the end, it comes down to individual preferences as well as to how serious you are. It may help you to know my decisions in selecting the equipment that I now own and use.

There is no question that the 35mm field has taken over most of the photographic market, and I myself own seven 35mm cameras. However, the 2¼ x 2¼ format is still my choice and should it come down to having only one camera it would be my Hasselblad. I have the 50mm, 80mm, and 150mm lenses as well as a 38mm for the Super Wide camera body. I can carry four magazines with twelve exposures in each. A Polaroid back lets me check composition, expression, and pose and *helps* in establishing the correct exposure. I stress the word *helps* because nothing guarantees the correct exposure. There is always some variation in batches of film or circumstances that influence the final outcome. So when I'm asked how one arrives at the correct exposure, I always answer, "You can arrive at only what you expect to be the correct exposure." Maybe that's the intrigue of photography—the suspense of never knowing the result until the film is developed.

As a professional, I must try for even more assurance that the skin tones and background are as close to reality as possible, so I use the following system:

After shooting one or two rolls with a model in a particular location using the same lighting circumstances on the entire roll (2¼ x 2¼), I label that roll #1. Then I put on a different magazine with the same type of film and expose one frame only in the identical location and circumstances. That magazine becomes my "test" roll. When I change location or model or lighting, I make another twelve exposures on a third roll. I label that roll #2. I now place the "test" magazine on the camera again and expose the second frame. Thus by the end of the session I will have exposed either one or two "test" rolls, each frame of which corresponds to the various numbered rolls. The "test" rolls are put through the lab first. I study the results knowing that frame #1 corresponds to roll #1 and frame #2 to roll #2, and so on. If the frame looks too light, I ask the lab to *shorten* the development time accordingly for that particular roll (usually by one-half stop) and if it looks too dark I ask the lab to *increase* the development time accordingly. Thus I feel that I can control the exposures with the maximum guarantee. Many professionals use this method. I am speaking of color film. With black-and-white film there is much more latitude and it is possible to make corrections when printing. The same holds true for color negative film.

Another factor in using the Hasselblad is that the ability to change backs without having exposed the entire roll enables me to shoot color transparencies one minute, change to black-and-white or to color negative, all of the same setup, thus giving me a range of choices for the finished pictures: prints in black and white or color, and transparencies for the client or my stock photo file.

I suppose one of my strongest arguments for the use of the 2¼ format is the ability to have portrait negatives retouched. I'm aware that many young people don't even know what retouching is, so for those of you in the dark, retouching is generally done on the negative—whether it is color or black and white. Small blemishes, freckles, and lines are worked over with lead pencils in capable hands and in the finished picture do not show up, giving the skin a smooth surface. It's obvious that the larger the negative, the easier it is to do this fine work. I've never known anyone who could retouch a 35mm negative; the image is just too small, even with a magnifying glass. In color transparencies, a different system is employed—mainly dyes—and this is much more costly than the work done on negatives. I am lucky to have found a talented person, Loretta Jackson, who is a retired photographer. She retouches my negatives, both color and black and white, and I've promised not to take advantage of her, by keeping the work to a minimum and her whereabouts a secret. While I've had good retouchers over the years, Loretta is by far the best.

My second-favorite camera is the 4 x 5 Gowlandflex. With it I do 90 percent of my commercial color work. I use the Hasselblad mainly for black and white. I built the first Gowlandflex in 1956 because there was no camera like it on the market. I liked the idea of seeing my subject right side up and also looking down into the groundglass as I had with all the Rolleiflex cameras. This gave me the opportunity, when working at the beach, to shoot from a low angle, which is difficult with conventional viewing, where I would have to practically lie on my stomach to achieve the same angle that I can easily achieve by looking down into the Gowlandflex. I am also able to hold the camera inverted and over the model by extending my arms above my head and looking up into the groundglass. Other cameras would require the use of a ladder to shoot from this height, about 7 feet.

I find that my clients prefer the larger transparencies rather than color prints or slides. Perhaps it is because I deal with lithographers who produce calendars and posters and with other companies who advertise with large cutout point-of-sale figures. With the Gowlandflex I am able to shoot a Polaroid, first making sure of composition, exposure, lighting, and posing. The Polaroid back, which takes the eight-sheet Polaroid pack film type 559, fits the Gowlandflex (as it does most view cameras) and is used for this purpose. Sometimes we take as many as fifteen Polaroids before we start with the regular film. On the average, however, it's more like two or three.

The Grafmatic holders enable me to take six exposures before changing to another holder. With this method I can send one sheet to the lab first, as with the 120 film, and run the other five sheets accordingly.

My second-favorite lens for black and white is the 150mm Sonnar f/4. I prefer it to the 250mm lens because it can be handheld. The longer the focal length, the more need for a tripod. The 150mm is also a faster lens. This picture was taken with the Hasselblad with 150mm lens on an overcast day; the filtered daylight is behind the model. We used a very bright silver reflector below the camera, as you can see by the large catch-lights in her eyes. The 2¼ negative can be retouched, whereas the 35mm negative cannot. This negative was retouched slightly. *Model, Marina Moore.*

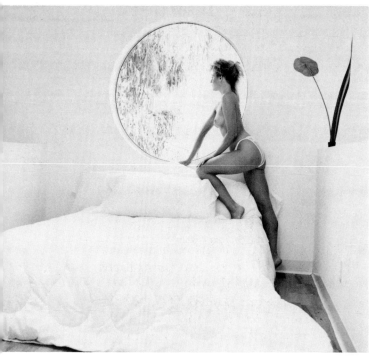

My third-favorite lens with the Hasselblad is the 50mm Zeiss Distagon f/4. It is good mainly in room situations. It is not a true wide-angle (about a 40mm); when I need a true wide-angle I use the Super Wide Hasselblad, which has a 38mm lens. This picture was taken with available light only in a modern home that had extensive glass and white interiors. When using available light indoors, I always use a tripod because of the long exposure time required. *Model, Debra Gaske.*

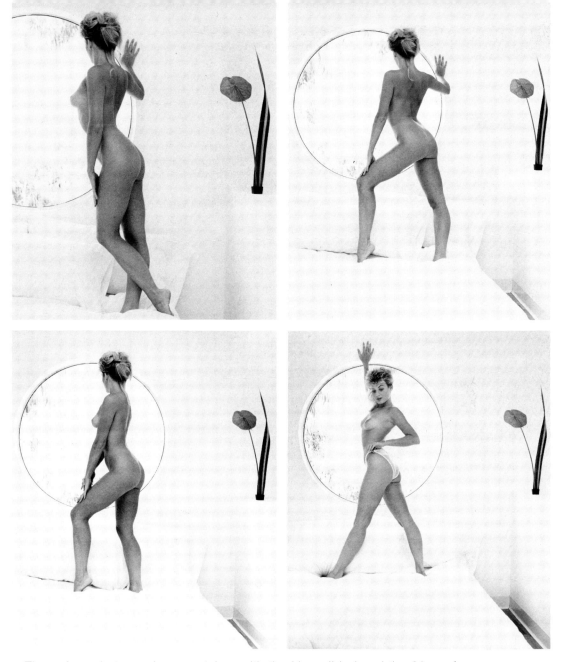

These four photographs were taken with the Hasselblad and the 80mm (normal) lens on tripod. *Model, Debra Gaske.*

What lenses do I use on the 4 x 5 Gowlandflex? In glamour photography most pictures are taken with a normal or longer-than-normal lens. For the 4 x 5 format a 150mm would be considered normal. However, I use a 180mm for most full-length and half-length poses. I find that there is less distortion with the 180mm or 210mm than with the 150mm. This is particularly true when the model's arms or legs are projecting toward the camera.

Occasionally I like to try something offbeat so I can lie on my studio floor with my Pentax and 17mm lens, which has some pin-cushion distortion as can be seen in the curved line of the floor—which is actually straight. I used two lights for these pictures: one on the background, camera left, and a second key light in a #2 position camera right. *Model, Iris Rounsaville.*

Hasselblad case. For twenty dollars I bought a used aluminum camera case, size 8¼ x 13 inches. I constructed a plywood divider that was nailed, glued, and then covered with red corduroy. The case contains the 500-C Hasselblad with 80mm lens, the Honeywell Strobosol, a professional lens shade (center), a Polaroid back, a Hasselblad standard lens shade with space inside for three filters, a Super Wide Hasselblad, a 50mm lens, a 150mm lens, two extension tubes containing a finder for the Super Wide Hasselblad. Bottom row, from left: three additional roll-film backs (12 exposures each), an electric timer for the Polaroid, a Spectra exposure meter, and an electronic flash exposure meter. The lid is lined with a 1-inch foam pad that keeps everything in place; behind the pad is a paper silver reflector that folds up.

The only other lens I prefer on the 4 x 5 is a 240mm or 300mm, and these are for extremely close facial shots. Long lenses are important for portraiture because they prevent distortion. The relative difference between the 2¼ camera and the 4 x 5 is that a 150mm would be used for heads on the Hasselblad but a 300mm or double would be used on the 4 x 5. Thirty-five millimeter cameras use 40mm as normal and 85mm as a portrait lens. A rule of thumb is to double the normal focal length when you move in for close-ups.

My third-favorite camera would be my ME Pentax. I should explain that there are two basic types of 35mm cameras, and it is important to know the difference. There are the single-lens reflex cameras and the rangefinder types. With the Pentax (reflex), which uses a mirror system inside the camera, I am actually looking through the lens when I put my eye to that little viewing area. The rangefinder cameras (Leica, etc.) require that two images (seen in the viewer) be brought together in order to be in sharp focus. The choice of which type you select will be up to you. The main difference is that with the rangefinder camera the viewing area always shows the same size image no matter what lens is attached. For example, if you are using a long, telephoto lens, you compose on a small frame in the center of the viewing glass but the finished picture will show only that small area, a close-up of that section. With the single-lens reflex, using the longer lenses, the subject is enlarged in the viewer to the same size that it will appear on the film. I find this single-lens principle easier and more comfortable to use. I must point out that Leica makes both the rangefinder and the reflex types.

The rangefinder is lighter in weight and has fewer moving parts because there is no mirror to move out of the way causing the split-second delay of the single-lens reflex. This split-second delay can be a problem when photographing action. The rangefinder is also quieter and does not warn the subject that the strobe is going off as is the case with the single-lens, which makes a sound just before the shutter clicks.

Because I like to be prepared for any event when taking a model on location, I carry my three different format cameras: the Gowlandflex, the Hasselblad, and the Pentax. The latter two have cases. I built the Pentax case of aluminum with wooden insets and lined it with red corduroy. I purposely eliminated the use of padding, except in the lid, because I wanted to keep the size and weight to a minimum. I am able to carry the two bodies and all the lenses and stow the case under the seat when flying. Although I have not been able to establish a list of clients who will accept 35mm transparencies for their assignments, I find that the Pentax's compact size and ability to use a variety of lenses inspires me to take more creative pictures than when using the larger formats. I've noted

Peter Gowland at the beach with model Suzee Slater, using his 4 x 5 twin-film camera with two six-sheet Grafmatic holders. This setup offers the possibility of shooting a color transparency and a black and white (or a Polaroid and a color negative) at the same time. Each film exposure can be set separately since two shutters are involved. A special double-cable release fires the shutters. Viewing is done through a sports finder.

The same twin-film camera is now used as a twin-lens reflex by looking through the top lens with a reflex finder; the film is being exposed by the bottom lens. Lenses can be interchanged with this camera. *Model, Suzee Slater.*

also that many celebrated photographers specializing in scenic and travel photography use the 35mm cameras exclusively. This format is also employed for editorial fashion photography where action is desired and a casual, natural background preferred. In commercial, glamour work where a product is usually involved or the photographs must be enlarged, sometimes to life-size, the larger film format is necessary. Most of my work falls into that category. The 35mm camera is very popular with

31

Model Tracy Rosenthal checks her lipstick in the mirror attached to the hood of the 4 x 5 Gowlandflex camera. A mirror is important when shooting on location when the model has only a small compact and has forgotten a larger mirror.

beginning photographers because it is less expensive than the Hasselblad or Gowlandflex, but one should know when seeking the higher-paying commercial jobs that the smaller formats have limitations. I'm sad to note that many 35mm fans haven't the foggiest idea of how to use a 4 x 5 view camera!

With my Pentax equipment I have the ability to photograph a subject at a great distance—using the 200mm or 400mm lenses—and sometimes even use a walkie-talkie to communicate my directions. The results can be quite spectacular because the telephoto lens can have the effect of compressing buildings, cars, waves, or people who may occupy the background. This can be accomplished by focusing on the subject and using small f/stops. On the other hand, these same objects can be thrown out of focus, thus making it possible to shoot a full-length figure against a cluttered background and not have it detract from the model's presence. In this case the f/stop would be as large as possible.

For close-ups of the model's face I switch to the 85mm and if I want to include her body I use the 50mm. Going to the opposite end of the spectrum I can achieve some offbeat distortions with the 20mm.

My main concern with 35mm is that with most of these cameras the use of the Polaroid is not an option—I'm so used to making that critical

Polaroid test before shooting. I know of one person, Dave Riddle, who modifies Professional Polaroid equipment for this purpose. His work is specialized, so you would have to write for information: Dave Riddle, 9400 Wystone Avenue, Northridge, CA 91324. Photographic labs, in some cases, will make a "snip" test of a 35mm roll and develop the balance of it accordingly. This is costly because the "snip" is usually charged at the same amount as a full roll. The 35mm cameras do not have the interchangeable back feature of the Hasselblad that enables me to load each back with a different film.

THOSE ONCE-A-YEAR CAMERAS

As professional photographers become successful and have more money to spend on equipment, they have a tendency to own cameras that may come into use only once or twice a year. I'm no different and have added to my regular outfits the following:

The Hasselblad Super Wide. This has a 38mm lens that gives me double the angle of the normal 80mm. I've had occasion to do architectural pictures for our local home magazine and after admiring the work of talented photographer Jeff Dunas, who places his gorgeous models almost incidentally in grand rotundas or on rococo balconies, wanted to try something like that. Finding the proper setting is 90 percent of the challenge. I have used the extreme wide angle with scenery and a model but the results were not nearly as spectacular as those mentioned previously.

The 8 x 10 view camera. I'm not keen about using the 8 x 10 format because it is tedious and requires great patience on the part of the model as well as the photographer, but the results are worth the effort when everything goes well and you have a *big* image to view. I use 8 x 10 mainly when I am forced to do so by the requirements of commercial jobs such as calendars or life-size cutouts or billboards. I also used the 8 x 10 on the eight centerfolds we did for *Playboy* magazine. With the 8 x 10 I use a 350mm lens, which is considered "normal" for that format. Depth of field is limited with long lenses. It is necessary to work at small f/stops (f/22 or f/32) in order to carry focus from the subject to the background. If the subject moves a tiny bit, she can be out of focus. The tilting lens board on the camera and the tilting back enable me to focus sharply on the face and feet. But what happens if the model is holding a glass that projects forward from her body? How can I keep that in focus as well? By using the smallest f/stop. The smaller the f/stop, the greater the range of focus.

But every time I reduce the lens opening by one stop, I must double the power of light that goes through it. Thus, my 800-watt-second power

Round-the-world Pentax case. I constructed this case of aluminum, welded at the corners. Wooden sections separate the various lenses and cameras: two Pentax MEs, 20mm, 50mm, 85mm, 200mm, 400mm lenses, extension tubes, and four extra rolls of film.

pack, which I generally use with 4 x 5, must be replaced by a 2000-watt pack. You might wonder if it is worthwhile to have such equipment when it is not put into use regularly. Well, it does pay off in the long run because 99 percent of photographers know how to use only the smaller formats, and the fact that I can produce beautiful glamour pictures with the large film gives me a greater edge when critical commercial jobs come along. That is why no camera is too big or day too cold for me to wade into the stormy Pacific and carry out an assignment.

Nikonos Underwater Camera. This brings me to my third "once-a-year" camera. This is the Japanese version of the Calypso, a French design. There have been many improvements to the Nikonos since I bought mine, but I have made successful pictures with it and continue to use it on special occasions. I took my first underwater pictures back in the late forties when I had the idea to photograph a nude suspended in the blue expanse of a pool. With the help of a machinist friend, who did the more complex metalwork and rubber seals, I built a box of plywood and glass to house my Rolleiflex, and with it produced some interesting studies of Joanne Arnold in poses that would have been impossible without the buoyancy of the water. I found that swimming pools must be crystal clear, with no sediment. There is a natural lack of contrast because of the

The Gowland Swing Light can easily be tipped up, down, or circle the studio. It eliminates the use of wires on the floor.

I designed this unit so that the umbrella light is always ten feet from the subject when the subject stands directly under the hub. There is enough space between the hub and the back wall to place backlights or background lights if needed. Two weights act as counterbalance to the umbrella light, which can be moved up or down or tilted around the studio. The umbrella is a 72-inch Larson Super Silver and I use it with a Norman 2000-watt-second strobe unit.

water density, so if the pool is cloudy the pictures will have no snap. I also found that I could improve the contrast by using an orange filter (with black-and-white film) and a CC red filter (for color transparencies). Contrast could be further improved by making black-and-white negatives from the color transparencies.

Once I am fond of a particular camera, I stick with it. I think this is good advice because if I were to change to a different make it would not be just the camera, it would mean an entire system. Kind of like getting a divorce—you have to change everything, not just your wife (or husband). There is an advantage to loyalty, in that familiarity with the technical part of a sitting leaves the mind free to be more creative. The photographer who jumps from one camera innovation to another loses a lot of time and never gains that oneness with his equipment.

FILM

Today there are so many film speeds to select from that one becomes confused. They vary from ASA 32 to ASA 1000 and up! Since I am a great believer in simplicity, I have selected the ASA 100 films for most of my shooting. If and when the occasion arises when I need a faster or slower film I make the adjustment. Making things even better, there is the possibility of using Fujichrome Daylite 100, T-Max black-and-white 100, and color neg 100. Thus when I am out on location it is fairly easy to change from one film to another without worry of a mistake in exposure. One meter reading or one Polaroid shot serves as a test for all films. I know that it is easy, when working fast, to put a back on the Hasselblad with color and the next with black and white and forget which film is being exposed. With the ASA consistent I can avoid errors. I haven't really attained this ideal status as yet but am working toward it.

For my 4 x 5 I use Fuji ASA 100 color transparency and sometimes Ektachrome ASA 64. The Polaroid 559 has a recommended meter setting of ASA 80. So I have juggling to do when making my tests and switching back and forth from color to black and white. The Hasselblad is loaded with Verichrome Pan or Plus X; both have an ASA 125. While all of these are close to the ideal "100 ASA," I'm still waiting for manufacturers to get together and decide on a standard ASA.

There is a formula that makes it possible to estimate your exposure for daylight on the ideal sunny day:

1. Set your f/stop to f/16.

2. Look up your film speed and set your shutter to that number. ASA 100 would give you 1/100, ASA 400 1/400, and so on.

On an overcast day you would open up one stop, to f/11. In the shade open two stops to f/8, and in very dark shade open three stops to f/5.6.

PROCESSING YOUR FILM

Color labs have become so numerous and specialized that I no longer process my own color film. I stick with one lab for the Fujichrome and another for color negatives. Becoming known by the people who run them gives me greater assurance that my film will be handled with great care, and occasionally they'll even extend themselves when I'm working to meet a deadline.

I've always enjoyed developing and printing my black-and-white negatives but when I have to print in quantity, such as with the photographic books, I'm frustrated in finding a printer who I feel has the same perception I do regarding what a proper print should look like, and who is neat in the darkroom. Alice is the only other person I know whom I can feel confident to turn loose with a batch of negatives and know they'll come out right.

We have two rooms, both 7 x 7 feet. Each room has a sink 30 inches x 7 feet and a bench 24 inches x 7 feet. The film room has a refrigerator for storing film and the printing room has four enlargers: an old Kodak Precision 35mm, condenser model; another old Kodak Precision 2¼, condenser type; a Bessler 4 x 5 condenser enlarger; and an old 5 x 7 Elwood diffusion enlarger that I bought back in 1938 brand-new for $25. I never use it now but, like my once-a-year cameras, it's waiting for that special job.

I recommend that photographers do their own darkroom work because they can always be in complete control, and should they want to exhibit prints as they improve, it's important that they do the lab work themselves. There's something quite restful and rewarding in watching a print develop and also in creating effects with various techniques (see chapter 10). But I am the first to admit that this phase of photography requires a special mood. I can never print on a sunny day!

FILING

I cannot stress enough the importance of filing your negatives and color transparencies *immediately* after you've developed and printed them. Before I turned professional I kept my negatives in glassine sleeves, but I really didn't have a system. Those negatives are still in a separate box waiting to be filed! But when Alice and I began making our living at photography, she insisted on a proper filing system. We decided to identify the negatives by the name of the model even when a company was involved. We made a separate book with each model's name and the highest number on her negatives. Each time we used her we knew where to start numbering.

In the case where we do a series of photographs that do not involve a model we use the company's name—and, here again, enter them in our green book along with the highest number on the negatives since we anticipate doing other work and would not want to confuse two jobs with the same series of numbers. By now we must have a half-million or more filed in a cabinet of wooden drawers; all are filed alphabetically for easy recovery.

All color is also filed under the model's name and here each transparency is numbered with the model's initials and a number beginning with 100. If the same initials belong to a different model we start hers with 200, and so on. A description of each color transparency is entered by number on a 5 x 7 file card and the transparencies are placed behind that card in a set of wooden drawers that hold the bulk of our color work. This file is constantly being cleared, whereas the black-and-white negatives are always retained. We clean out our color file every five or so years because $2\frac{1}{4}$ x $2\frac{1}{4}$ and 4 x 5 color take up a greater amount of space than do the strips of black-and-white negatives. We eliminate images that appear dated due to hairstyle, costume, or makeup. If a particular transparency has appeal even though dated, we save it in a file labeled "older color"; these are filed by the year in which the photograph was taken. We occasionally get requests from advertisers or property departments of motion picture studios who need pictures from a specific era. This "older file" is a source for this situation.

All models' proofs are filed alphabetically in a standard 8 x 11 metal cabinet. Our favorite pictures from each session become part of a catalog system which we print by the thousands and send to advertising agencies to generate business. We are now up to catalog xii. Photographs in the catalogs are numbered consecutively from #1 to #3801 (our latest). Negatives for these pictures are separated from the model's file and put in a special box containing all catalog negatives. Thus if a client orders #301, we can easily find it. All $2\frac{1}{4}$ x $2\frac{1}{4}$ negatives are cut in strips of four and all 35mm negatives are cut into strips of five, making them easy to handle in the darkroom.

The catalogs are also sold to photographers as "posing guides" for five dollars each. We've kept them at the same price for years! The idea for this came when a photographer stopped by my studio and asked if he could buy one of the catalogs to show his model. Later he called to say what a help it had been in suggesting poses for her to copy. Incidentally, one should never worry about copying. The same idea with a different person in a new setting will take on its own personality. Nothing in this world is original anyway.

We still have some of these catalogs available if anyone is interested. Just write to me at 609 Hightree Road, Santa Monica, CA 90402.

In our driveway, which is off the main road, I was able to make this indoor setup. First I laid a carpet, then added a box that resembled a window seat, and with the help of some poles and a sheet covered the set so that the light was soft sunlight. I had built a glassless framework that acted both as windows and a wall.

3

OUTDOOR
GLAMOUR

Glamour photography does not require a studio. The biggest, freest set of all is at the disposal of anyone who wants to take advantage of it: the great outdoors! My first photographs of women were made using beaches, parks, and private property. I still prefer these same outdoor backgrounds to studio setups.

No two days are ever alike, weatherwise, so one has to observe and remember the difference between bright sun, bright overcast, dark overcast, and shade, and how these variations affect photography.

Coordinating weather conditions with your own shooting schedule is one of the aggravating aspects of outdoor glamour work. Even though I work in southern California where it is supposed to be forever sunny, that is not the case.

BRIGHT SUN

When the sky is blue and the sun is bright I do one of two things: head for the beach or put up a paper roll in my patio. Chapter 11, on synchro-sun, covers the beach and other locations where electronic flash is used, so here I will extol the beauty of strong, dark shadows as cast by the noonday sun and how these can be effective when used with a white paper roll. The two subjects that lend themselves to this simple setup are the nude and fashion. It is not absolutely necessary for the model in either nude or fashion shots to look into the camera, so that shadows, of interest on the body and clothing, are avoided on the face by directing it

upward, toward the sun, or away in profile. This system is the simplest setting for a photographer to learn in lighting the figure without the use of expensive equipment. The sun, acting as a gigantic point-source, illustrates dramatically the effect of light and shadow. I've used this technique mainly at noon because in most cases I do not want the long shadows cast by the late or early morning sun to cross the background.

BRIGHT OVERCAST

Green fields, open streams banked by foliage, glens, all lend themselves to this diffused sun, when a fine haze casts only the faintest shadows. This condition can produce beautiful images. In most cases no additional source of light is necessary, but if the subject looks directly into the camera, a soft reflector or small flash can add a touch more light to the eyes. Remember that although it is a broad, diffused light, it is still basically a "top" light—the most unflattering to the face. My color transparencies on these days are restricted to backgrounds other than the sky because of its great expanse of white.

DARK OVERCAST

My wife, Alice, and I disagree on this subject. She likes the results of this moody top light. I find myself aggravated, trying to compensate for the lack of illumination. The use of reflectors is almost worthless since

These three photographs were taken with filtered sunlight but the main source of light for the face was a silver reflector. Hasselblad with 150mm lens. A Polaroid was taken after using a Spectra Incident Meter to determine the exposure. *Model, Marina Moore.*

By shooting down at model Karen Witter, I was able to make use of the grass and shiny leaves as a background, with Karen using the tree trunk as a backrest. Hasselblad with 80mm lens and a Norman 200-B electronic flash from the #1, front, position.

there is very little light to reflect. Whether I use color film or black-and-white, and fill in with flash, the pictures have an allover gray quality. Some advertisers like the somber ambience this heavily overcast sky creates, but I haven't yet learned to like it.

SHADE

There are two types of shade: open shade and dark shade. Open shade is found under overhangs of buildings where light surfaces can cast reflection onto your subject or where it is possible to use a white sheet, white cardboard, or silver reflector. To use this type of shade without the benefit of added light is not flattering. The natural color of shade is blue; therefore, a gold source of reflection can add warmth when photographing with color film. With black-and-white film there is no appreciable difference between the gold and the silver.

Dark shade is found in heavily wooded areas where the dense growth of trees blocks most of the light. Fine art photographers love this. They take long exposures and find joy in reproducing green tones of ferns and rocks. But in glamour work this locale restricts the model to holding still for long periods of time. Results of combining this natural beauty with a feminine touch can be spectacular or just not come off at all. I personally have not had success with this setting. But I'm sure it is a possibility and certainly admire those who find it a challenge. Reflectors here do practically nothing. Flash lights the subject, but the backgrounds remain black. Two flash units, one directed from the front and one used as a backlight, will do wonders for the subject, but make it pointless to work in such conditions since the forested areas behind her are lost to darkness.

Any dark, covered areas where there are no reflected surfaces to lighten them should be avoided when it comes to glamour, as far as I'm concerned. My personal preference is to keep the background as simple as possible because my model is to be the star. Anything else should complement and not overpower her. For that reason I am always on the alert to possible locations, even when I have no particular photo session in mind. I store these images away for a later date. Take, for example, a parking lot raised above the sand at our local beach. A bank leads down to the beach and at certain times of the year is covered with small yellow flowers. When I noticed these I stopped my car, studied various angles through my camera and at a later date photographed Teresa Ring on a towel, with the sparkling water behind her and a few of the flowers in the foreground. One would never guess that she is just inches away from some sad-looking asphalt. I made use of the same location again, with a different model and different angle. This time I went down the bank and looked up against the sky. It was perfect for Stephanie Drake, seated as though she were on a country hill.

A most unlikely place to photograph a nude against the sand was a park that we came upon while driving around with our model. Naturally

This picture lends itself more to color than to black and white, and I include it here to illustrate that fact. Most photographers that I speak with think that foliage is great as a background, but only if it's backlit will it work at all. Even so, I prefer a plainer setting. Hasselblad with 80mm lens and a Norman 200-B in the #1 position. *Model, Caroline Stone.*

Model is framed by an ivy-covered archway. Personally, I would have preferred the background to be clear. Another shot that would have been better in color. *Model, Caroline Stone.*

By shooting up at model Stephanie Drake, showing the blue sky, we make it appear as though she is on a mountaintop. She is actually sitting on a bank covered with yellow flowers in a parking lot near the beach. A yellow-green filter was used on the 80mm lens of the Hasselblad. The sun was in the #4 position 3/4 rear, right side, with a Norman strobe in the #1 position near the camera.

this was not on a weekend because there were no people using it. A brightly colored jungle gym, by the look of it recently installed, was situated in the middle of a circular sandbox filled with refined white sand. The platforms of the play rig served as a vantage point for my camera. I used a tripod because the day was dark overcast. At first I posed the model in a bikini and then, when we realized how insulated we were from the public, it was easy for her to slip out of her bikini top and do some seminudes. This location proved to be great for a miscellaneous group of portraits, action shots in a swing, and some sultry poses on the slide.

What I'm saying here is that, even though this appeared to be a cluttered area when we first saw it, only a few minutes of close inspection through the camera lens convinced me that we could work around the distractions by using either a high or low angle. So don't discount any location until all points of view have been explored.

I seem to be a majority of one when it comes to praising wooded areas as backgrounds. These are the disadvantages that I could find:

1. It's difficult to locate clear areas against which to pose my model. I've overcome this drawback in many instances by using black space, rather than white sky. In other words, by putting the sun behind her, the green foliage photographs as black because it has no light hitting it.

2. The light level is generally low and is usually top light, which is so unflattering. I've solved this problem by using flash or reflector to work as a front, key light on the model. This way I have control of the direction and intensity of the key. I prefer the electronic flash because reflectors are too bright for most of my models and cause them to squint. In case I haven't mentioned it before, holding a reflector high so that the reflection of the sun shoots down at the subject seems to be less offensive to the eyes. (Chapter 11 covers this in detail.)

3. The color green absorbs light at a rate of two stops more exposure than normal, so in the finished picture, unless the sun is hitting the foliage directly, the green never looks as brilliant as it does to the naked eye. I've solved this problem by using a sheet, which my assistants hold high over the model, to protect her from the direct rays of the sun. Although this gives a soft, top, shade light, I am able to modify it by using an electronic flash from the front. The background, however, is bathed in sun and thus the foliage retains its true color.

The advantage of living near wooded areas is that there is generally a lake nearby and it is possible to use the water as a beautiful and changing background for your model. A large body of water is not necessary. You need only enough to surround your model. Trees that grow around the lake can be used as props if they are close enough to the shore so the

Yellow flowers growing at the edge of a beach parking lot make a good setting for model Teresa Ring. The sun on the water produces a nice sparkle. Hasselblad with 80mm lens; Norman strobe lights face from the #1 position. The sun provides backlighting.

On the same parking lot strip, in the same lighting situation, I switched to a 150mm lens and moved in for a close-up. The background is now out of focus. *Model, Teresa Ring.*

subject can hang on to a branch and lean out over the lake, letting the water be the background and the tree the frame.

Now let's explore the enjoyment of photographing at beaches and lakes. For me there has always been a magic quality about water whether it's still or active. At our local beaches, we sometimes have huge waves and at other times the tide is way out, leaving expanses of wet, reflective sand. I've learned, through experience, not to let the magnitude of a scene distract me, and acknowledge that only a portion of the whole will be necessary if I want the model to be the center of attraction. If I'm after a fine art print, then I may use the model as an incidental part of the overall view. In commenting on photographs that are sent to me for my critique, I can easily spot where the photographer has become over-whelmed by the scene because he has tried to capture both the expanse and the girl at the same time, which doesn't do justice to either.

I like to take advantage of the water's movements, so I use the beach mainly in the summer when the water is warm. In winter, when the sun is bright but the ocean's temperature is below 50° F, I carry along plastic bottles of hot water so that after my brave model poses in the shallow surf I can revive her by pouring this over her body.

The churning foam creates a natural reflector, so when I am posing a girl in the surf I must be careful to take this added light into account and adjust the exposure accordingly. For example, if I have posed a model on the wet sand and have arrived at my exposure either with a meter or Polaroid shot, and then take the picture when the foam has returned, it may be from one-half to a full stop overexposed. So it is wise to take the picture under the same conditions that the test exposure was made. If you do not have a flash, this foam condition can provide enough reflec-tion on your model without the use of any additional light.

You'll notice that most of my beach pictures are taken with sun and electronic flash. I feel this is the most flattering to the model and I use the flash no matter what the time of day—even at sunset. The sun, as it hits the foreground or background, will make the pictures take on a different appearance; for example, late in the day with the sun behind the model and with the camera aimed down at the shallow waves, the water sparkles, whereas earlier in the day the same wave may be white and foamy.

Rocks are great as props but I personally prefer one at a time rather than a cluster. I still resort to using a group when I cannot isolate one from the others, but a single rock keeps the model's figure clear of distractions. A single rock makes a better target for a wave, the resulting spray fanning out in myriad patterns. These chunks of gray or moss-covered configurations lend themselves to sitting, leaning, or kneeling poses.

When photographing clothing, I look for interesting architecture with open shade or sun and having tones in pastel colors for the walls. I usually get permission to work on or around the premises (sometimes shopping malls are good locations if they are small), and aim for times when the stores are not yet open. Stairways, glass walls, chrome pillars all lend themselves to working with fashion models. These locations all require the photographer to work fast and in the early morning hours. Those two circumstances would be the main drawbacks.

By cropping the negative we were able to remove the distractions of the background, filling the frame with the model and letting just a bit of the tree add to the outdoor feeling.

High on a bluff, overlooking the beach, a fence makes a nice prop for Teresa Ring to lean on. Strobe on camera in #1 position. Overcast day allowed no sun to hit model.

On a bluff overlooking the highway, Teresa Ring poses on a fence and is framed by the leaves of a tree. This picture is of historic interest because visible in the background is the rigging where Occidental Oil plans to slant-drill sixty wells! On the Pacific Coast Highway yet! Lighting was one strobe, on camera (#1 position), controlled by the f/stop. Background of hazy sky was controlled by the shutter speed.

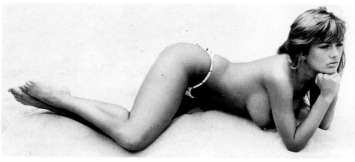

Peter Gowland holds his Gowlandflex 4 x 5 camera inverted over his head and looks up into the groundglass in order to photograph a model posed in a reclining position on the sand below.

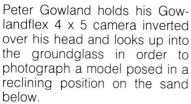

These were all taken from a jungle gym at a local park. A high angle made possible the use of a space that otherwise would not work as a background. Here, although the sand at the park extends no farther than shown at the top of the picture, it would appear to be part of a beach. The day was overcast and I used Plus X to gain contrast and overdeveloped it by 2 minutes in D-76. Hasselblad with 80mm lens at 1/125 at f/8. Natural light only. Model, Linda Johnson.

Overcast day at a local park, with no people around, made it easy to photograph model Linda Johnson posed in a white teddy. The sand made a smooth background. Overcast days are great for moody black and whites but tend to be blue and cold when color film is used. Hasselblad with 80mm lens; natural light only.

With the 400mm lens on the Pentax, I stood about 20 feet away for this portrait of Linda Johnson, using the Pentax on a tripod because of the longer exposure time needed to compensate for the low light. My assistant stood close to the model with a bright silver reflector to get as much light as possible onto her face.

Linda leaning against the posts was shot from the top of the jungle gym about 40 feet away. Pentax with 400mm lens on a tripod.

Flash is in two different positions in these two pictures. In the first picture we held the flash close to the camera, low, so that when model Linda Johnson swung Into focus (peak of action), I clicked the shutter and fired the strobe. In the second picture, my assistant held the flash high. The flash in both low and high positions was necessary for shooting against the sky on an overcast day; without it Linda's face would have been dark and not detailed. Hasselblad with 80mm lens, 1/500 second.

The following pictures were all taken at the beach, with a Norman 200-B strobe on the camera in the #1 position, with the sun acting as a backlight. Hasselblad with 80mm lens.

Low afternoon sun creates sparkle on the water in this "puppy" pose. Rocks as an outline are fine, but the one rock directly behind model Caroline Bartlett intersects with her body in a distracting way. I had hoped the wave would cover it.

Using rocks again for posing gives model Stephanie McLean a natural support for showing off her lovely figure. Her left leg extended adds length to the pose.

In winter, when the ocean causes erosion, sandbanks form that make interesting backgrounds or supports as the sun creates shadows evocative of the Grand Canyon. *Model, Kerry Fotre.*

Nancy Fletcher has the California girl look, healthy but trim, with a beautiful face and figure and a naturalness when posing in the surf. Hasselblad with 80mm lens. Norman 200-B on camera in #1 position, with sun coming from the #5 position.

Nothing is more striking than a white foam background contrasting with a bikini-clad figure. Here, model Nancy Fletcher walks toward the camera, her leg kicking up the shallow surf.

A wet T-shirt breaks up the monotony of the bikini and, in this case, the torn T-shirt fad takes on the same pattern as the foam background. *Model, Suzee Slater.*

This was taken as a stock photo shot for our files. Couple strolling on early morning beach after a night party. Early morning sun on left adds highlights to the dark complexions and a flash fills in from the #1, front, position. *Models, Alretha Baker and Alex Marks II.*

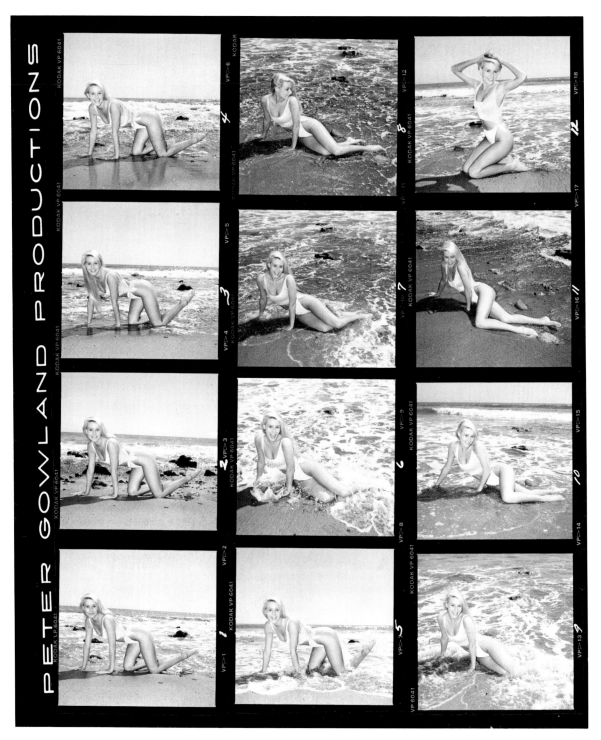

A typical proof sheet taken at the beach using a Hasselblad with 80mm lens and a Norman 200-B strobe. Both high and low camera angles were taken to ensure the most flattering background and pose. In photos 1 through 4, rocks were distracting but the tide covered most of them in 5. Both 5 and 9 were selected for printing. *Model, Heather Ley.*

INDOOR GLAMOUR

Plain studio backgrounds, using either paper or the curved wall, never thrill me, except for silhouetted or partially silhouetted nude poses. But many of my clients require this uncluttered setting, either for covers, posters, fashion catalogs, or ads, so I have learned to work in this style with pleasing results by placing emphasis on lighting, posing, selection of model, and, sometimes, special effects (see chapter 10).

Many poster companies prefer the model to be photographed either in a compact seated pose or standing, cut off just above the knees. That's because they want to fill as much space as possible with girl, leaving only what is necessary for their printing. Full-length poses, while showing the entire body, show a smaller image of the model, with space around her.

CREATING SETTINGS IN THE STUDIO

With "boudoir" photography becoming so popular all over the country, many portrait and wedding studios are being swamped with requests from wives and nonmodels who want sexy pictures of themselves. I'm told they want them either for their husbands or boyfriends, or just for posterity. At any rate, this new interest in glamour pictures of women of all ages and occupations has created a challenge for those who generally only do portraits. The ages of these subjects can range from eighteen on up! The pictures can be taken indoors or out, but the majority that I've seen are studio shots, taken with dark backgrounds. Photographers who specialize in boudoir photography tell me that there is somewhat of a formula. The subject decides on how much nudity will be shown, and generally it is merely a shoulder or a back, or the body revealed through a see-through garment, but always executed in soft, diffused lighting conditions that suggest rather than show nudity. I've tried a few of these pictures by using a black background and draping the figure in white lacy fabric, and using a #3 Harrison & Harrison filter over the lens. (These are described in greater detail in chapter 10.) It's important that the eyes look directly into the camera, as though addressing whoever will be seeing the picture. With one subject, I used a white background with mylar on the floor, letting the nude figure be seated in a quiet pose, not looking at the camera, and with some of the background lights spilling off onto her body. The key light was from the #3 (side-light) position, thus keeping the skin tones dark, in semi-silhouette.

An alternative to the black background is to create a bedroom atmosphere in the studio. In many ways I prefer this to working in the crowded area of an actual room. The studio affords space to back away from the model without fear of showing ceiling lines. Another advantage to building a bedroom setting is that only those props relative to a feminine atmosphere need be added. Calendar clients usually ask for these romantic-looking surroundings, and when the format required is vertical it's quite possible to crop close, leaving only the portion of a prop as a suggestion. However, the request now is for a finished transparency that can be used either vertically or horizontally, and that means the composition of the picture leaves space at either side of the subject that has to be taken up by a plant, a pillow, a bedpost, or whatever, and frankly limits the pose. I prefer to make the original picture either one way or the other for a much more pleasant composition.

I either move a real bed into the studio or use the floor, against the window, filling the space with a satin quilt and many pillows to assume the appearance of a bed. There is always an artificial look to these sets and I think it comes from the need to keep the background perfectly plain, with just a hint of additional furniture on the edges. The lighting for the calendar nude is generally a #1 (from front) or #2 (from 45 degrees to the side). The main areas of concern are the face and the breasts. The light at the #2 (45 degrees) side position gives a shadow to the bosom and by turning the model's body slightly it is accented even more. Her face, on the other hand, should turn toward the light for the most flattering appearance.

USING ACTUAL ROOM SETTINGS

One might think that it is less trouble to use an actual bedroom or sitting room than to create one. In some ways this is true; however, ceilings are normally 8 feet high and that restricts the angle of view and the distance from which the photographer can work. Also, in room settings furniture must be moved to allow space for lights. Conditions become quite crowded. I always recommend using soft lighting in room settings, which can be achieved by bouncing the lights from the ceiling and using others bounced onto the model, rather than placing strong direct lights on the background and on the subject. I think, from looking at pictures sent to me by aspiring glamour photographers, that one of the main problems with working in actual room settings is that the average bedroom furniture is not particularly attractive and there is more than likely a television set, a clock radio, and piles of books, all distracting from a glamorous setting. These photographers put too much emphasis on looking at the model and do not notice what goes on behind her. My advice is to get rid of those ordinary objects and replace them with something more feminine—a jewel box, perfume bottles, a vase of flowers, or better still, hang a lace curtain by means of a rod suspended between two poles. If you happen to have a bedroom or sitting room that opens out onto a patio, it's fairly simple to place your camera outdoors and shoot into the room, leaving more space between you and your model. Direct your camera in a more downward angle, say, at eye level, if the model is in a seated pose. Usually in all seated positions I shoot down on the model because this is more flattering to the breasts and face. But if she is standing (which is rare) I place the camera at her waist level because any higher would make her legs look shorter.

In summary, I would say that the background should be related to what the model is dressed in; keep it simple by eliminating unnecessary pieces of furniture, add feminine accessories only, and keep the lighting broad from the front, separating her from the background by using a hair light, any light placed above the model or to the side/above and directed at the hair. The background itself takes up about ten times the space that the subject does, so it will require from one to four lights depending on the mood of the picture.

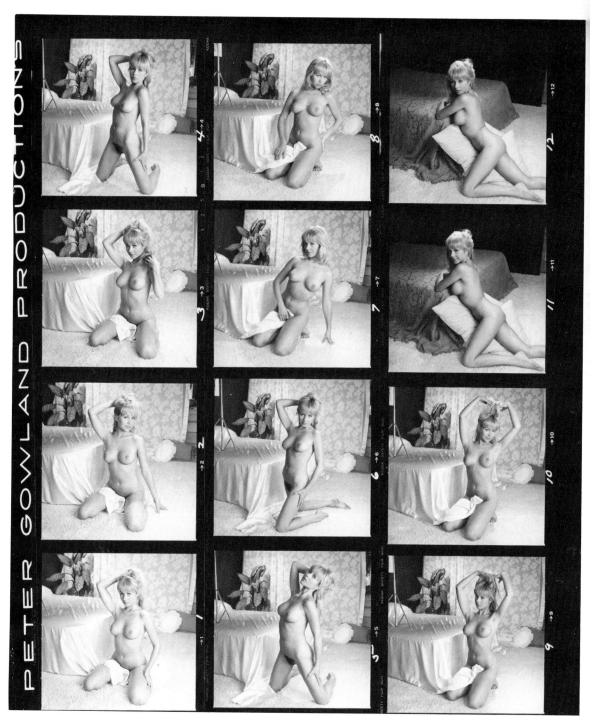

Proof sheet showing the same room with a change of bedcover and furniture to create two different settings. We picked numbers 3, 4, and 8 as our favorites. *Model, Alexandra Day.*

62

Change the look of a bedroom by putting a satin sheet over the bed, hanging a curtain (cover drawers and a TV set), throwing in a plant and a couple of pillows. Even though the model was facing an outdoor patio in which the photographer had placed his camera, little or no light from this source was picked up by the film. The main light source was a Larson Starfish 48 inches from camera right in the #2 position, which accentuated the shape of the breasts. Another light was used to brighten the background. This is where most amateurs fail—they don't light the background. One hair light (a small 50-watt-second flash on a boom) was also used. This is a typical calendar-type picture, which has model in feminine setting, looking into the camera. Black and whites were taken with Hasselblad and color with the 4 x 5 Gowlandflex using 180mm lens. *Model, Alexandra Day.*

Suzanne Copeland models for a Gowland seminar of ten students. The day-light studio is shown with a 72-inch Larson Hex being used as a key light and the 880 Highland Honeywell Strobonar lighting the background.

Here, a bedroom setting was created by placing a mattress next to a window in the studio and a throw pillow in the background. This is also a popular calendar setting. In the studio I have more space to work in and am in control of the lighting, in this case two 36-inch translucent umbrellas with two Strobosols coming through them from a #2 position on the left. Light on model's shoulder is from hair light at the #4 position (top and back). Black and whites were taken with the Hasselblad using 80mm lens and color with the 4 x 5 Gowlandflex using 180mm lens. *Model, Debra Gaske.*

Creating calendar settings in the studio for speculation and our stock photo file, we used mattresses and pillows with satin sheets and a screen with a plant to further give the impression of a room. In black and white this setting takes on a rather flat tone but in color (blue background, light blue sheets) the skin tones are complemented. The background is lit separately and the key light is a 72-inch Larson Hex at a #2 position, attached to the Gowland Swing Light for quick changing from one side to the other. *Model, Ferosha Nibarali.*

Use of curtains hung in the studio suggest "boudoir" and today that is very popular with women who want to give their spouse or boyfriend a sexy picture that really does not expose too much. A light in a #3 position comes from the right and leaves most of the body in shadow. *Model, Christine Abbott.*

Here, the light is coming from the #3 position left, giving light to the body and casting moody shadows on the face. Background behind curtain is lit with a second flash unit. *Model, Christine Abbott.*

Typical "boudoir" photograph shows model posed against dark background with a #3 light from the left and a #4 from the right. The key (#3) is a Larson 72-inch Hex and the #4 is a direct flash (Larson Strobosol). This was shot through a #3 Harrison & Harrison diffusion filter with a Hasselblad and an 80mm lens. For added intimacy, model looks into camera. *Model, Shelly Winnaman.*

A set built in the studio consists of boards for flooring, a black background, and two swinging doors. To get the smoke effect we had an assistant take puffs from a cigarette and blow it into the set before each exposure. The lighting was a #2 from the front right and #4s from the rear on the right and the left. The two background lights were direct and the key light was bounced. *Model, Linda Gordeuk.*

Indoor setup using silver Mylar on floor and a couple of rocks in foreground. Most of the light is on the background, but the two background lights (one on each side) spill over onto the model slightly, which keeps her figure dark with a minimum of highlights. Mylar creates an effect similar to using water, but the presence of a seam defeats the illusion. *Model, Shawna Roebuck.*

The simplicity of this shot makes it a typical poster or calendar picture. The natural look of the model is appealing. The color scheme was a light purple background with varied shades of purple for the teddy. The key light is between the #1 and #2 positions, with a #4 lighting her hair. Four other lights evened out the background. Black and white was taken with Hasselblad using 80mm lens; the color was taken with 4 x 5 Gowlandflex using 210mm lens. *Model, Karen Witter.*

Using only the light from the window and a Larson 36-inch Super Silver reflector, this 2¼ x 2¼ negative is the compromise nude. It is not the graphic *Playboy* nude, yet it is not too covered. A low reflector is in the #2 position. Hasselblad with 80mm lens. *Model, Linda Johnson.*

To let the action take place in the background, the model stands still while a slow shutter speed of 1/30 or 1/15 second is used. Here, the Pentax with 200mm lens on a tripod was placed at a distance of about 30 feet. The use of a longer lens would bring the car closer to the model. *Model, Linda Johnson.*

5

ACTION

Here's the one type of photography that takes luck into consideration. One never knows how the finished picture will turn out when the subject is going through a series of dance movements, jumps, or is running along the beach. So, be prepared to use up lots of film.

It seems to me there are four types of action: (1) passive, (2) posed, (3) peak, (4) spontaneous.

I consider a wave, splashing in the background, as passive action. The model is required to do nothing but look pretty—the water adds the motion. The photographer has the choice of whether the splash looks blurred or is stopped, clear and sharp, depending on his shutter speed, which could be 1/30 for the blurred action to 1/500 for the stop action.

Objects that move across the background also fall under passive action because, here again, the model assumes a pose and either cars or people move in streaks behind her. The slow shutter speed of 1/15, which will cause the objects to blur, requires the use of a tripod, and my model must hold perfectly still in a predetermined pose until after the shutter clicks. The use of a long lens, such as a 200mm on a 35mm camera, will appear to bring background objects closer to the subject but more out of focus than would a normal lens.

The wind, blowing the hair, dress, or scarf, is also a passive action that brings life to fashion or portrait studies.

Still another example would be using water from a garden hose, backlit by the sun. Here again the model depends on a second element to provide the action. Water is best shown against a black background. Outdoors this could be any area that is not receiving direct light.

Posed action is used with dancers, fashion, couples, or portraits. A dancer may go through a series of positions until the photographer sees one he likes. She will not move out of the predetermined composition but will strike the pose just before the shutter clicks, or she may hold the pose. Either way, the result will look as though she has just completed an action or is about to start one, giving the impression of motion. A couple walking on the beach is a posed form of action because the photographer instructs them where to stop and sets his camera on that focus. They then go into a slow stroll so that at the time the shutter clicks they will have stopped, but with the appearance of motion. A pretty face, turned away from the camera, head spinning around at the last minute, gives posed action to a portrait. The hair has a slight swing to it, unlike when a fan is used. A posed action in fashion would be one in which the model is stationary, facing away from the camera much the same as with the portrait, and turns at the last minute, causing the dress to flare.

All of these posed action pictures require several exposures to be sure of getting one that is perfect. None of the subjects move closer or farther away from the camera; the shutter speeds are from 1/250 to 1/500.

Peak action requires that the photographer have a sharp sense of anticipation. It takes a bit of practice. The model rehearses a movement, say, a ballet leap. The photographer studies it and memorizes where the peak of the action takes place (the point at which the model stops going up and begins to come down). The dancer goes through the movement and the photographer clicks the shutter a split second before she reaches that point. The split second before is particularly important when using single-lens reflex cameras, where the mirror has to move out of the way before the shutter fires. I take at least twelve to twenty-four exposures on each bit of action to ensure that I've anticipated correctly.

A couple jumping for a ball or a gymnast on a trampoline also fall under this peak-action formula. Working in my studio I use my more powerful electronic flash unit for this particular phase of action. An interesting point is that with small strobe units that fire as fast as 1/10,000 second one can stop the action, but the light is weak and does not carry to the background. With the heavier units the light is strong but the speed may be only 1/200 second.

So, when employing my Norman 2000, which fires at 1/200, I must rely on my shutter speed to stop the action. With my Hasselblad at 1/500 this is possible. However, I am using less than half the light because the strobe is slower than the shutter. Most 35mm cameras synchronize with electronic flash at only 1/60 to 1/100, so the action cannot be stopped completely if shooting under studio conditions where electronic flash is necessary. However, outdoors, using daylight, some of the more professional 35mm cameras have the capacity of 1/1000 or more shutter speed and can freeze the subject and motion beautifully.

The following photographs were all taken at the beach with the Hasselblad, using 80mm lens (normal) at 1/500 second (the top speed on the Hasselblad).

← The camera will stop the action of a person running toward the camera better than it will the action of a person running across the path of the camera. Note that the model's hand, moving across the plane, was not able to be frozen. Lighting here is sunlight at the #2 position, adding cross-light, the sun, to model's chest. The picture is approximately a 35mm section cropped from a 2¼ x 2¼ negative. *Model, Melissa Prophet.*

A low angle was used to get as much sky as possible and also to make the girl (5 feet 3 inches) appear taller. High sun from the left with flash fill. *Model, Stephanie Drake.* →

Complete backlighting by the sun plus flash on camera combine to give this "posed" action shot an allover washed-out appearance. *Model, Tita Moore.*

Spontaneous action is where the subject is running either toward the camera or across the field of vision. In this situation it is impossible to know just exactly where her arms and legs will be in the finished picture and that is where luck comes in. I have noticed, over the years, that a model running toward the camera looks better if her legs cross each other slightly rather than having a space between them, so I ask my subject to concentrate on trying to achieve this. Still, we must go through the action again and again to ensure one frame that we both like. I pre-focus on a distance where I anticipate the most pleasing configuration of her form will be by having her run slowly through the action first. Then, as she runs toward the camera, I just hope that her legs and arms are in those same pleasing positions at the time I fire the shutter.

Action crossing the camera is the most difficult to anticipate. Generally I place the camera on a tripod, focus on the model at a particular distance, then have her back up and run across the frame. Looking into the finder and waiting makes it almost impossible to anticipate, so I try to guess by watching her with my naked eyes. A second method is to pan with her action. In this case the background could blur but that needn't spoil the picture; in fact, it might add to the effect.

Motor-Driven Cameras. You may notice a consistent thread running through my philosophy of photography: simplicity. I usually shy away from excessive mechanical sophistication because I feel there are too many factors that can go wrong. But having purchased a Canon A-1 with a motor drive (because it was such a good buy), I had a chance to try it out. I must admit that I was impressed with the results. However, one must be prepared to go through a lot of film. Remember, this gadget can move a maximum of 5 frames per second so in a matter of seven seconds I had finished a roll! It can also be set at 3.5 frames per second or on single frame. This motor drive, used with action that is approaching the camera, will see the subject move in and out of focus so that not all frames will be sharp. However, when panning with the action there is no problem. I've read that the newest Canon cameras with the automatic focus ability will yield only 3 frames per second.

Posed action where model holds the predetermined pose and lets the wave create the impression of action. Flash on camera in #1 position with the sun from behind. *Model, Jilanne Leigh.*

Rehearsed action with a couple. Photographer predetermines distance and composition, then models jump into it at his command. Notice how the female model is able to show her body to the best advantage by stretching it and pointing her toes at the same time. Lighting is provided by flash on camera, in #1 position, and the sun at noon, which is usually a bad time, but with models in action and looking up, it doesn't have an adverse effect here. *Models, Stephanie McLean and Clark Coleman.*

Rehearsed action becomes spontaneous when wave is more forceful than anticipated. Model Alretha Baker jumps back to avoid getting her dress wet, making a better picture than the one planned of her walking. Sun at high noon, with Norman strobe. *Model, Alex Marks II.*

Couple rehearse walking toward camera with sun behind them. Flash on camera in #1 position. Shutter is snapped when they reach a prefocused point. *Models, Alretha Baker and Alex Marks II.*

This picture was taken in a public park. With the sun in the #3 position, giving cross-light to the figure, a low angle was used to give as much clear background as possible. Camera was almost touching the pavement. Although focus was rehearsed, model Lisa Greer was coming so fast that her hips were in focus but her head went out of focus. When using the fastest shutter speed, it is necessary to use a large aperture, which does not carry depth of field. A yellow-green filter was used to darken the sky. Hasselblad at 1/500 second; Norman 200-B on camera in #1 position.

The following three pictures use water for action. Taken with Hasselblad with 80mm lens at 1/500 second.

Model in wet suit is posed first to feature legs and cleavage, then shutter is snapped when wave hits. The action of the waves is enhanced by striking the rocks. The sun is in the #4 position with the flash in the #1 position, on the camera. A yellow-green filter was used to darken the sky and protect the lens from the saltwater spray. *Model, Shelly Winnaman.*

With the sun hitting no part of the background, the green foliage appears black, making the white water stand out. Care must be taken when working with water to protect the camera from the unpredictable spray. This can be achieved by using a long lens or a filter over the lens. *Model, Heather Haines.*

This picture was taken in the patio around noon. A black felt flat frame (6 by 6 feet) was propped up to hide the garden. The sun was in the #4 position (3/4 camera right), a reflector in the #4 position camera left, and a strobe in the front, #1 position. I had three assistants on this: one on the hose, one with the reflector, and one holding the strobe. *Model, Bettina.*

A typical proof sheet showing the various exposures used. This sheet is a consolidation of the 24 pictures taken for this session. Negatives are cut in strips of four and are laid, three strips at a time, in a printing frame in contact with the same type enlarging paper used for the 8 x 10s. Name in Litho Negative is taped inside the frame for easy identification. *Model, Shelly Winnaman.*

These five pictures were all taken in the studio with the Hasselblad and 80mm lens at 1/500 second. The 72-inch Hex Swing Light was placed at 45 degrees left of camera (#2 position). There were four Larson Strobosols on the background to wash out any shadows that the key light might cast. The 1/500 shutter stopped the action while using only half the amount of light.

Model Shelly Winnaman is a professional dancer so was able to attain considerable height in her leaps. When white backgrounds are used, as in this case, white can be added in the darkroom to the top or bottom of a picture to increase the illusion of height. This wasn't necessary here because all action was rehearsed to establish where the "peak" took place.

These two pictures were taken with the 72-inch Hex Swing Light at the #2 or #3 position.

When using a white costume on a white background it is necessary to place the light to the side (#3 position) in order to create shadows so that the model will stand out. Even so, the left leg is lost to the light. It would be better to use a darker shade in the costume. *Model, Shelly Winnaman.*

Light here in the #2 position helps separate model from white background, giving a poster effect by outlining her body with a fine black edge. Four lights on background, one on model. *Model, Shelly Winnaman.*

The following five pictures were all taken with the Hasselblad and the 80mm lens. Four Strobosols were used on the background and the Swing Light was in the #1 position in the front. The model was wearing dark clothing, which separated her from the white background.

Gymnast Jill Osborn is able to stand on her toes without the benefit of shoes! Jill is the type of model I enjoy working with because she is full of energy and talent. The photo below illustrates that the 1/200-second duration of the heavy-duty strobe was not successful in stopping the action on the entire body. Leg that came up in fast motion shows movement. Actions were all rehearsed to establish peak.

These were taken with the Hasselblad, using the 80mm lens.
Mylar was used on the floor in a
conventional room setting where
the bottom edge of the wall,
meeting the floor, is apparent
and somewhat distracting. One
disadvantage of Mylar is that it
wrinkles very easily at the touch,
creating a jagged reflection,
whereas water doesn't. *Model,
Lesley Heasler.*

These three pictures were taken with the Pentax, using a 55mm lens, in the studio against a curved background.

When you have a ballet dancer with imagination and talent she can create original poses. Here, she finds an unconventional way to sit on an antique piano stool. Four lights on background, none on subject. *Model, Iris Rounsaville.*

Here again, the unconventional pose, in ballet costume, gives an original stamp to an otherwise typical picture. A #3 light from the right and four lights on background. *Model, Iris Rounsaville.*

The old "flipping the head" trick. Model lowers her head and swings it up on cue from photographer. Many exposures are necessary to catch the hair in a flowing motion. The four lights on the background spill over onto her body, with another light at the #3 position. *Model, Iris Rounsaville.*

These two pictures were taken with the Hasselblad. Four lights on the background, with the 72-inch Swing Light coming from the #1 or #2 position.

Our daughter, Mary Lee Gowland, an aerobics teacher, does a leap for us in a costume that stands out against the white background. With exercise as popular as it is in all areas today, this type of picture is good for a stock photo file.

Earl Chapin and his wife, Clara, two aerobics teachers, show their exuberant good health and agility in this pose taken as an ad for Earl's Health Gym. Hex was in a #2 position, which gives definition to the muscles.

These four pictures were taken with a reflector and daylight, using a 500-C Hasselblad with a 150mm Sonnar lens, Verichrome pan film. An unconventional approach to the standard photo of model and swimming pool. Here, model, lying on a deck, dips her head in the pool. A reflector catches the late afternoon sun and reflects it back onto model, who is in the shade. **Model, Kelby Anno.**

With weak sun overhead and model in partial shade of a tree, the reflector is placed between model and camera, just below the camera. *Model, Marina Moore.*

Garden setting with backlighting on overcast day. Reflector kicks in light from camera left. *Model, Karen Witter.*

Alexandra Day posed in a bedroom using a tiger rug to add a touch of fantasy.
Camera was positioned on the patio, shooting into the room. Three lights were
used. The key light was a Larson 27-inch Soff Box at the #2 position camera right.
A second light was used on a boom above the model to light the hair. The third
light, a tungsten bulb, was used on a stand behind the model, giving a yellow cast
to the edge-light on her hair. Exposure was adjusted to 1/10 second to accommodate the tungsten light. The f/stop was set to allow for the Larson Soff Box. We
used a Norman 800-watt-second power pack and the Gowlandflex camera with
Ektachrome film.

The key light here was a Larson 27-inch Soff Box in a #2 position camera right. The second light, a small Honeywell 880, was directed onto the background camera left. The third light was a small 50-watt-second portable strobe. Gowlandflex camera with 210mm lens, Kodak Ektachrome ASA 64 film. *Model, Christine Abbott.*

A bedroom setting created in the studio, lighted by four 36-inch Larson translucents with four Strobosols as the power source, two on either side of the model. A light on an Ascor boom illuminated her hair. One must be careful when using a hair light that it does not strike the nose or cheeks of the model. The light should be placed back, aimed toward the front and blocked from hitting the lens by using a go-bo. Gowlandflex 4 × 5 with 180mm lens and Fujichrome film. *Model, Linda Johnson.*

A stained-glass window behind model with sunlight coming through at a #4 position camera left. A blue filter over a 1000-watt quartz light provided illumination from a #2 position. To balance the sunlight with the tungsten lighting, a dimmer was used to control the quartz light. Pentax ME with an 85mm lens and Kodachrome ASA 64 film. *Model, Marilyn Hamilton.*

This double exposure was made by first photographing the block of ice against a black background, and saving the film. We also made a Polaroid test to help us set up the second exposure. This second shot, of a model alone, was also against a black background, with red cellophane over the two backlights. The Gowland Swing Light was at a #2 position camera right. The block of ice was photographed with sunlight and reflectors to bring out the edges. Gowlandflex camera with 180mm lens and Fujichrome film. *Model, Shelly Winnaman.*

Typical cover or calendar pose and lighting. The Gowland Swing Light with the Larson 72-inch Hex was in the #1 position, with one hair light from above (Ascor 200-watt-second), and four lights (two on either side) on the background. Gowlandflex 4 × 5 camera with 210mm lens and Fujichrome film. *Model, Audrey Bradshaw.*

A local home, waiting to be sold, was the setting for this picture. Available window light only; no additional light was necessary. Hasselblad with 80mm lens and Fujichrome ASA 100 film. *Model, Debra Gaske.*

We took this picture in an actual bedroom but changed the color scheme by putting a colorful bedspread on the wall, pink sheets on the bed, and adding orchids. Lighting at the #1 position next to the camera was a Larson 36-inch Soff Box with a Norman 800-watt-second power pack. A light on the Ascor boom served as a hair light. It could have been placed a touch farther back to avoid having it hit the shoulder. A Strobo-sol 880 was used to light the background camera right. Gowlandflex camera with 4 × 5 Fujichrome film. Space was left on sides so picture could be cropped for vertical or horizontal use. *Model, Ferosha Nibarali.*

On the Gowland patio a black felt flat was propped up to provide the background for model Alexandra Day. A shower head attached to a hose was directed at the model by an assistant. The sun came from the top and a Norman 200-B strobe on the camera was in the #1 position front. Reflectors were used from the left side at the #2 position. Gowlandflex camera with 210mm lens and Kodak Ektachrome film.

A high angle affords a simple background of grass with midday sun. Shawna Roebuck was asked to tip her head back and close her eyes to avoid ugly shadows on her face. Hasselblad with 80mm lens and Fujichrome film.

The terrazzo floor adds its reflective qualities to this picture of model Shawna Roebuck. There were four lights on the background: two Larson Strobosols on either side. Any light on the model was from the edge of these lights; there was no other illumination. Hasselblad with 80mm lens and Fujichrome film.

This picture was taken with window light only. Hasselblad with 80mm lens and Fujichrome film. *Model, Linda Johnson.*

This picture was taken with natural lighting only at around noon with the sun directly overhead. We used the 8 × 10 Pocket View camera with the 300mm Schneider Symmar lens and Fujichrome ASA 100 film. The 8 × 10 camera takes a little time to set up, so we had the model pose in a bikini first since we were on public property. After taking a Polaroid shot with the Hasselblad to establish that everything was as we wanted it, we quickly had the model remove the clothing and took at least four 8 × 10s and a few 35mm in a matter of 3 minutes. *Model, Shawna Roebuck.*

A block of concrete, part of a storm drain, suggested a pose to Stacy Alden. Notice that she kept her toes pointed. Sunlight was at a #4 position left with the key light, a Norman 200-B, in the #1 position on the camera. Gowlandflex 4 × 5 with Fujichrome film.

Shooting from a high angle, the sand is prominent, so it is important that it look smooth. We waited until the water had receded before making this exposure. A colorful umbrella serves as a prop. The Norman 200-B strobe was on the camera in the #1 position. Gowlandflex 4 × 5 with 180mm lens and Fujichrome film. *Model, Caroline Stone.*

A pretty, young face that looks perfectly natural by the application of subdued makeup. Photo was made by use of the Larson 72-inch Hex on Gowland Swing Light placed at a #2 position to give slight shading to face. Below chin, between model and camera, a Vari-Flector by Smith-Victor was placed on a stand in a flat position to bounce the key light from this low angle. Note double key lights in eyes. Ascor boom light from above lights the hair; one light on background. Hasselblad with 150mm lens. #3 Harrison & Harrison diffusion filter. *Model, Therese Hallquist.*

A black background is usually my favorite for a portrait because I can use backlighting. Three backlights were used here: one from the top; one from either side in the #4 position. A front light, the Gowland Swing Light with the Larson 72-inch Hex, was in the #1 position. Hasselblad with 150mm lens. *Model, Lisa Greer.*

Girl with flowers is a calendar theme that has persisted for many years. Usually the request is for a girl with roses. One has to be quick when working with the tight-budded flowers because they bloom right before your eyes! The Gowland Swing Light was used from the front in the #1 position with a Honeywell Strobonar at camera left to give added light to the flowers. Greens and reds always require more lighting than other colors. The hair light came from the #4 position camera left. *Model, Margaret Shumar.*

In a public park it is difficult to find a clear background but by lowering your camera angle it is possible to use the sky instead. Hasselblad with 80mm lens, with the Norman 200-B strobe on the camera. *Model, Lisa Greer.*

A studio shot with black background and backlighting. Four backlights (Larson Strobosols), two on either side, were in the #4 position, and the Gowland Swing Light with the Larson 72-inch Hex was in the #1 position, front. Gowlandflex with 210mm Symmar lens and Fujichrome film. *Model, Shelly Winnaman.*

6

PORTRAITS

Portraits are probably the easiest type of glamour photography in one sense and the most difficult in another. Dealing only with the face eliminates having to pose and light the rest of the body, but no amount of flattering angles or lack of shadows can make up for a bad expression. So it's up to the photographer to put his subject at ease and to know when to click the shutter.

I'm lucky in that I enjoy people and I'm interested in knowing what they like to do, so I find it easy to talk to my subjects. Also, when trying to be an actor in my youth, I was painfully shy in front of a camera (still am), so I sense that immediately in others. When I'm working with girls from agencies, those who have had a considerable amount of modeling experience, I find they're surprised at my gift of gab. They don't know quite how to react when I ask them what their boyfriend's name is, or how long they've been married or what their astrological sign is. Most of them laugh when they say they don't have a boyfriend or aren't married. I see them give Alice an oblique look as though to say, "Is this guy serious?" But I've accomplished my purpose—to make them relax. Even these professional people have a touch of nervousness, and in talking with them during or after a sitting I find out that their experiences with many studios have been very sober with little time for small talk. Being serious is something I'm never accused of, and while I've noted looks of anxiety on my clients' faces, they needn't worry, because my mind is never far from f/stops and shutter speeds. Once they see the results they're no longer dubious.

I purposely do not have all the lights in place when my model is ready. I like to have her sit and watch as I fiddle with things that really aren't important, a tactic that many dentists use to distract their patients. Getting people to talk about themselves automatically starts them on a diversionary road from their own insecurity. Flattery is the greatest tool of all, but it has to be sincere. I'm surprised at how many pretty models really are not aware of their specialness and, anyway, praise is something one cannot overdo.

What I'm saying here is that 90 percent of the success in working with models depends on the photographer's personality and the ease with which he works. That is why I stress the importance of learning technique so that it becomes almost automatic, leaving the mind free to concentrate on the enjoyment of the moment.

PORTRAIT POSES

Now that the subject is relaxed and over her fear of failure, it isn't at all difficult to suggest that she lie down on her stomach, using the bench or floor—whichever is more comfortable. I'm amazed at how many models have never been asked to assume this position for portraits, and sometimes they think I'm kidding. The reclining position provides the following advantages:

1. Not only is my model more relaxed, she *looks* relaxed.
2. The reclining pose—on her stomach, horizontal propping herself up with her elbows, face turned toward camera—enables the photographer to work the arms and hand into the composition more easily.
3. The subject cannot move about readily and thus keeps in frame and focus.
4. Reclining poses tend to pull the neck muscles, tightening them for more flattering pictures.

This does not mean I never seat a girl in a chair. I do. In this case I study both sides of her face and have her turn one way and then the other before deciding which side is best. I usually take both sides if it's a toss-up. On those rare occasions when I can't find a good angle, I tip the model's head to one side, letting the hair fall forward and having her hands rest on a stool, out of range of the framing.

In my studio I have a plate glass mirror 32 x 48 inches on casters that takes its position next to my camera so the subject can make sure the photographer doesn't miss anything, such as a hair out of place or a wrinkle in the clothing. Many photographers don't like this idea because the model may have a tendency to look into the mirror at the last minute, but I don't find this to be a problem because I work slowly and warn the model when I'm about to shoot.

OUTDOOR PORTRAITS

A good starting place for portraits is the great outdoors. Owning a camera that takes long lenses is important. If your normal lens on your 35mm camera is 40mm, I suggest you double it for flattering portraits. Using the standard 40mm or 50mm will cause distortion if the camera is close enough to fill the frame with the model's head. The longer lenses will allow for a close-up while the camera is at a distance from the subject, preventing noses from appearing larger than in reality and ears from shrinking back. To avoid distortion when using 2¼ x 2¼ cameras, I recommend the 150mm focal length. For a 4 x 5 format, I recommend the 300mm.

The most flattering outdoor portrait lighting would be bright shade, where there is reflection from a wall or building. Lacking this, a silver reflector can be used. I frequently use a gold reflector because shade lighting is on the cold, blue side (it comes from the sky rather than from the warm sun). The gold reflector should be placed in the sun and directed at the model, bringing a warm glow to the otherwise cool shade. The reflector should be soft gold if it is to reflect the sun, otherwise the model will have difficulty looking into it. If, however, you are using it to reflect the shade lighting that does exist, it will need to have a bright gold surface. A mirror will often serve as a reflector under these low-light conditions.

MODEL AND REFLECTOR IN SUNLIGHT

I don't recommend the use of a reflector when you are posing the model with the sun in back of her and are hoping to fill in the face by using the reflector. It is impossible for the film to handle the extreme ratio between the highlights and shadows. In other words, her hair, backlit by the sun, will be ten times overexposed compared with the light on her face from a soft reflector. Why not use a brighter reflector? Because she could not tolerate the bright light in her eyes. That is why I use electronic flash when these conditions occur. With strobe, the model does not have to face this uncomfortable brilliance and I can cut down the exposure of the sun backlighting the hair by using a faster shutter speed and at the same time build up the flash as much or little as I like by using larger or smaller f/stops.

These pictures were taken with 150mm lens on the Hasselblad, using Norman 200-B electronic flash near camera, with sun backlighting the models and a reflector to one side. Verichrome pan film, developed in D-76.

Stephanie McLean and Clark Coleman find it comfortable to pose on soft sand in the shade of a catamaran. The boat helped to eliminate the glare from the sand and acted as a sun shield to the camera.

After posing for several full-length pictures, model Suzee Slater relaxed in the shallow surf. Reflection from the white foam helped light the chest and face, but the main source of front light was the electronic flash. The 2¼ x 2¼ negative afforded slight retouching on the face.

SOFTENING THE FLASH

Flash is a point-source of light, casting very hard shadows, not unlike the sun itself. How do you make the flash soft like a reflector? Easy—use a translucent screen between the flash and the model. My answer is the Larson 18-inch translucent. You can use one as a main light, near the camera, or you can do as I do, use two—one on each side of the camera. I have mine mounted on a 25-inch aluminum bar so that there is just enough space for my Hasselblad professional lens shade to fit between the two. The bar is attached to my Quick-Set Tripod (vintage 1955) with a 1/4-20 thumb bolt. When I pick up the tripod, I am picking up the camera, two strobe heads, two translucents. I can easily move from place to place. The two Norman strobe heads are connected to a Y-cable, plugged into my Norman 200-B battery power pack, which I carry over my shoulder.

I try to set up in the shade because if the sun hits the two translucents, they set up a reflection that causes my model to squint. I look for a location where the sun backlights her body. With easy calculation I can

Comparison of pictures taken with flash or reflector

Taken with sun in back of model. A reflector was used to lighten the face and a #3 Harrison & Harrison diffusion filter was placed over the lens. The extreme contrast between the sunlight on the hair and reflector on the face was impossible to record within the limitations of the film. The decision was made to expose for the face and let the hair become overexposed. The diffusion filter accentuated the overexposure even more but created an unusual angelic quality. Shooting with the lens wide open also increased the effect of the filter. *Model, Caroline Stone.*

Same place, same backlighting, same lens and film, but a smaller f/stop (f/16) was used, which made the hair sharper. No diffusion filter was used in this photo, and the exposure was correctly balanced between the sun and the flash. This is the more commercial of the two pictures. The 2¼ x 2¼ negatives allowed for slight retouching.

balance the strobe light with the sun. Here is a chart of my exposures, which I tape to the angle bar for quick reference:

Two Translucents 18″ with ASA 100 Film Using 200-Watt-Second
Norman Strobe
4 feet f/11   6 feet f/8   10 feet f/4.5

The f/stop controls the power of the flash, while the shutter speed is set according to the brightness of the background. In chapter 11 on synchro-sun, I mention that foam at the beach might require 1/400, while shade or the light near a window could require an exposure as slow as 1/8

92

Using translucent diffusion outdoors

Actress Corinne Calvet's netted, wide-brimmed hat tames the sun and makes interesting patterns on her dress. A Harrison & Harrison #2 dot filter creates soft facial planes and highlights on the hat.

When I want to have complete control over outdoor lighting and the subject is in the sun or has sun in back of her, I set up the equipment in the shade. That way, the person posing does not have to look into the white translucents with the glare of the sun hitting them, and I get the softest light possible on both sides of the lens. The tripod supports the Hasselblad with 150mm lens and a bar, bolted to the tripod, which holds two Norman heads connected to a Y-cable. The cable is plugged into the Norman 200-B strobe. The sync cord connects the camera shutter to one of the heads and both lights fire simultaneously through the 17-inch Larson translucents. *Model, actress Corinne Calvet.*

second. You will have to work out these various background conditions according to your particular combination of film and strobe. The flash exposure can be estimated with a flash meter and the background can be read with the conventional light meter. Usually I bypass the tedious metering and calculating by using a Polaroid color 559 for the 4 x 5 camera and a Polaroid color 669 for the 2¼ x 2¼.

BLOCKING THE TOP LIGHT

The sun at midday provides the most unflattering portrait lighting. It shines straight down, hitting the top of the model's head, highlighting the nose and leaving two dark holes for eyes. This "top" light, as I call it, is used in motion pictures when the aim is to produce a depressing effect on the audience. This brutal technique can be modified by using scrims. A scrim can be a white sheet, a translucent piece of plastic, or even a dark screen, anything to keep this top source from doing its damage. At the beach, an umbrella will do the trick. We had one couple pose under the canvas bridge of a catamaran that had been pulled up onto the soft sand. The light from my Norman 200-B became the key light from the front position. There was no squinting, the models were comfortable on their stomachs, and my strobe performed its usual magic.

There are exceptions when top light can give a very dramatic attitude. One example would be when the subject tips her head back and closes her eyes as though enjoying the sun. Another is the bodybuilder who wants to emphasize the ripples he or she has worked so hard to get. The problem here is that the body may look great but the face may look rippled, too! A reflector or even a strobe carefully directed to cover just the facial area can counteract this effect.

WATER PORTRAITS

I enjoy taking water portraits as a break from the conventional. Often I pose the model in the wet sand and have a wave wash in around her. This gives a bit of action to a static picture. Other times I pose the model up to her neck in a swimming pool so that her body is submerged with just her head on the surface. Using this same technique, the late Don Ornitz, a most imaginative photographer, made history with a water portrait: his model's beautiful face and wet hair were surrounded by a pool of gold! He achieved this by hanging gold cloth across the pool and shooting down toward the model. He was careful to crop out the cloth, leaving only the reflection showing. Since I feel that trying another person's idea is flattery and usually results in something quite different, I plan to try this technique myself.

INDOOR PORTRAITS

Window light, just the way Rembrandt used it, is a popular setting for many TV commercials today. The face and body are lit only by what comes through the window. To the naked eye the picture may look perfect, but if no additional lighting is provided, the contrast between the sunlit area and the shadow side is so great that the film's limited latitude cannot capture what the eye sees and the result is most unflattering.

This harshness can be modified by using an electronic flash either direct or through a translucent screen. In lieu of a screen, the strobe can be bounced against a number of surfaces: a sheet, white cardboard, a silver reflector, a wall, the ceiling. Remember, though, that ceiling is top light and might not be as flattering. On the other hand, because of the side-light from the window it might work out okay. You could also cut down the sunlight by using a gossamerlike curtain. If the day is overcast, the light from the window will be soft already and you can use a silver reflector or mirror to fill in the shadow area slightly. The degree to which the shadow side is softened determines the moodiness of the picture. It's best to use several techniques while you have the setting ready. Even blue photofloods will serve the purpose.

STUDIO LIGHTING

The use of too many lights, the most common misuse of studio lighting, causes conflicting shadows on a face or body. I cannot emphasize enough the principle that *one* light should be the *main source* and can be used successfully without additional illumination. If you want to learn portraiture from a graphic standpoint, begin with *one* light, and you will be able to see where shadows fall at its various positions. All other lights that are brought into the sitting should be subordinate—in other words, of lesser strength so they do not create new shadows but fill in where the key light has left darkness. A wide light source, such as the Larson 72-inch Hex, spreads the reflected light over a greater area than would a spotlight or direct strobe light, so any shadows that are cast due to the position of the Hex can be delicately filled in by using an additional source—which can be another strobe placed farther away from the subject and directed toward the shadow area. Too often a photographer places one light on one side and another of the same strength on the other, and the result is a conflict of shadows on the face.

In my studio I use a 72-inch Super Silver Hex umbrella that swings around the room in a 10-foot arc. Since it is counterbalanced, the light can be positioned high or low and automatically stays wherever it is placed. Wires feed from the Norman head, through the hollow tube of

The following pictures are typical of the Gowland studio setup for portraits.

Peter Gowland adjusts Vari-Flector from Smith-Victor so that it will pick up the light from the Larson 72-inch Hex Super Silver. A Norman 2000 using 1200 watt-seconds is the source for the flash. The hair light above the model is an Ascor 200 watt-seconds on a boom. In back of the model, directed toward the background, is an old Honeywell Strobonar Auto 880 Pressmaster (see if you can find one!). We adjusted the bracket so that the light could be tipped to the configuration of the model's figure so that she conceals the light and stand from the camera. A mirror, placed behind the camera, allows the model to see herself. The Hasselblad is set up on the Gowland camera stand. Gowland hardware for the Swing Light allows the 72-inch Hex with strobe to revolve in a 10-foot circle around the model. The Hex with strobe also raises and lowers by means of counterweights. Notice that this setup provides model with a view of a garden instead of the closed-in walls of the studio. Hasselblad with 150mm lens; Verichrome pan film, developed in D-72. *Model, Amie Johnson.*

Portrait taken with the same setup as in first picture. We have model Kerry Fotre standing, leaning over a stool to get a nice neck and head angle. When using a 6-foot reflector, one light (from #1 position) will usually suffice; however, a hair light definitely gives the picture more snap. Slight retouching on negative. The Gowland Swing Light was used.

Key light in #1 position with two lights coming from behind in the #4 position, one on either side, separate the dark hair from the dark background. This technique of placing brunettes against black backgrounds is one I use frequently. Gowland Swing Light was used. *Model, Alretha Baker.*

Same model with a different hairstyle in front of a light gray background. One hair light from above; Gowland Swing Light. *Model, Alretha Baker.*

Light at #2 position casts pleasing shadow to nose and cheek. One light on the background; Gowland Swing Light. *Model, Sharon Carlson.*

Same single Hex light at #1 position gives a flat illumination to the face. Reclining position enables model to use her arms in posing. One hair light and one front light; Gowland Swing Light. *Model, Karen Witter.*

A #1 light from the front with two backlights at #4 position (45 degrees rear). One of the #4 lights is striking the cheek and nose but in this case does not detract from the portrait. No diffusion. Hasselblad with 150mm Sonnar lens; Gowland Swing Light. *Model, Ava Lazar.*

the umbrella stem, out the top of the umbrella, up to the end of the ceiling pole to the hub in the center of the room. From there they go across the ceiling to the 2000-watt Norman power pack. With this system there are no wires to get in the way when shooting. The light can be swung from left to right, high or low.

When I am photographing a model for her portfolio and she needs a portrait, I always have her face the key light. Her body may be turned away from that direction, but her face should receive the full benefit of the bounced light. This washes out unflattering shadows. When I'm working for a more dramatic portrait, I may place the key light to the side, leaving half her face in shadow but knowing that retouching is going to be necessary because of the cross-lighting effect on the faintest crease or wrinkle. Only the very young models can stand this combination of shadow and light. When Alice and I first began taking portraits we used lights rather than strobes. That was what most of the photographers of the "stars" used. The results were beautiful, exciting, and we were able to make ordinary-looking people who came to us for portraits feel as though they were glamorous. We used "hard" spots, which cast black shadows. A second "broad" or a small spot was used near the camera to soften these brutal shadows, but we were always careful to place this second light as close to the camera as possible so as not to cast a second shadow. Also, we used the services of a talented retoucher. All of the old Hollywood-style portraits depended on retouching.

Today, with the use of the broader light sources, retouching is sometimes not necessary or is cut to a minimum.

Even though I may start with *one* light, I improve my portraits by using additional "fill" lights, a hair light, a background light. But I am always careful to watch those shadows, making sure that if one light casts a shadow, the other washes it out, or diffuses it.

Some of my most popular portraits were made with black backgrounds. In this situation I may use as many as four backlights, all directed toward the model from behind. I must be careful that they do not hit her cheeks or nose if she turns her face. I also may station a light directly behind her head, pointed toward the camera. This makes a halo around her hair when the lights are flashed. Her head protects the lens from flare from this source.

Also, I have found out through trial and error that "flare" can result when too much light is used on a white background. My theory is that a long lens is like a pipe—there is more inner surface to reflect. So in using long lenses for portraiture, keep the background light to a minimum. A single light behind the model, directed to the background behind her, will separate her from the background and give a nice gradation from very light to darker on the edges, calling attention to the subject in the center.

Three portraits of Hollywood actresses taken with #1 light (from front) and a reflector below the lens that picks up the key light and bounces it under the chin. Hasselblad with 150mm Sonnar lens; Gowland Swing Light. All taken with net diffusion.

The black background enabled us to use a Honeywell Strobonar 880 behind, and directed at Corinne Calvet's head, thus creating a halo effect on the hair.

Comparison of angles, diffusion or no diffusion, retouching or no retouching, backlight or no backlight

Having model Shawna Roebuck turn her head from one side to the other guarantees finding the best angle. In this picture we used a Harrison & Harrison #1½ diffusion filter. No backlight was used and we did not retouch the negative.

Ann Palmer, taken with a 36-inch Larson Soff Box above the camera, a reflector below the camera, and one hair light. One light was added, on the background, in the second picture.

With the head facing in the opposite direction the nose and the expression in the eyes immediately look better. A Harrison & Harrison #3 diffusion filter was used, which helps to cause halation, adding white to a gray picture. A backlight (from #5 position) was directed toward Shawna's head. A tripod supports the Hasselblad and a bar with two Larson 17-inch translucents through which two Norman heads fired at 100 watt-seconds each. The Norman 200-watt pack supplied the power. *Retouching, Loretta Jackson.*

A picture that does not reflect the work put into it

With model Linda Johnson lying on a window seat, there was not enough light coming through the glass to lighten her hair so we added an Ascor boom light above. From the front we had a total of four 36-inch Larson translucents with four Larson Strobosols firing through them, two on either side of the camera. This produced a very flat light with no shadows and eliminated the need for retouching. Hasselblad with 150mm lens, Verichrome film.

$\longrightarrow$

In contrast with the last two photographs, this one was taken with only the hard sunlight coming through the window, late in the day. Hasselblad with 150mm lens. No retouching required. *Model, Shelly Winnaman.*

I try to avoid shooting down in a full-length shot because it tends to make the model look shorter. Shawna Roebuck is petite, about 5 feet 2 inches. This was taken with the Pentax, 50mm lens, on T-Max Kodak film. The only lighting came from the window (#4) and from the door (#3).

7

P O S I N G A N D A N G L E S

POSING

Posing does not come naturally to everyone and many times I am surprised when interviewing a prospective model, someone who has expressed a desire to follow that career, to have her admit that she hasn't the slightest idea how to stand, sit, and so on. Invariably it follows that she is a passive person, one who has not taken up dancing or sports. Her pictures will reflect this and there is really no way of changing her personality to that of one who is able to move and arrange herself in pleasing, energetic poses. You can help her by showing her pictures from magazines or from your own file of other models who tend to be static. In photographing her you will have to think languid. Plan situations and backgrounds where she is not expected to show animation. For your pictures of this girl to have impact, your imagination will have to work overtime in creating interesting lighting effects, backgrounds, costumes. Also, her features and figure must be outstanding because there is no movement to cover up imperfections and fool the viewer. I've worked with this kind of girl both with pleasure and with aggravation. It all depends on her flexibility. If she is graceful, it is easy to rearrange a hand placement, or gently move a leg or foot. But, if she is awkward and just plain lazy, with leaden movements, then it's tough going and *only* if she is extremely beautiful would I take the time to photograph her. In today's sexually oriented markets, appealing to a youthful audience, this type of subject is frequently seen slouching in the backseat of a car, sitting on a bench, pouting, never smiling—not really the model I'm used to working with, but necessary once in a while to add variety to the life of the photographer and to his portfolio. Challenging, too.

By lowering the camera to approximately Shawna's waist level and coming in closer, she's made to appear much taller. Lighting here is the light coming in from the door in #3 position and from the window, #4 position. Pentax with 50mm lens on T-Max Kodak film, with camera set on "Auto" exposure.

These two pictures of high and low angles show that the high angle features the face and the low angle features the legs. The lower angle gives a clearer background. Pictures were taken at a local park on an overcast day. Pentax ME with 200mm lens, on T-Max Kodak film, with camera set on "Auto" exposure. *Model, Linda Johnson.*

The idea is to go along with what your subject projects rather than cause ill feelings by trying to make her into something she is not. Dancers, for example, pose themselves. They are generally full of enthusiasm and need very little directing. They can also be passive since they are graceful by nature, so it is a bonus whenever I find a dancer/model. I first photograph her in action (see chapter 5).

Example of high and low angles. With the camera above eye level, model Shelly Winnaman's torso is featured. With camera at her hip level, her legs are featured, and she looks taller. A rule of thumb: When a horizon line is involved, it will reveal the elevation of the camera. Both pictures were taken with the Hasselblad, using the 80mm lens and a Norman 200-B electronic flash in the #1 position on the camera. The sun hit the model from camera right, at the #4 position.

Even if a model appears to be at ease when getting into positions, there are things to watch for that she would not be aware of, and I'm speaking here of bikini, leotard, negligee, and nude classifications. I generally pose the body before worrying about expression or tilt of the head. Concentrate on seeing the waistline; don't hide it by having an arm close to the body or by having her lean too far forward. Women who have no waist but have small hips, a more boyish figure, must be turned slightly side-view to add the look of a curve, a waistline. Women who are thick in the middle should be photographed front, with last-minute instructions to suck in their waist. Weight that is carried in the hips or upper thighs can be hidden by several means: posing on the knees in high grass, with the hips turned slightly away (provided that the subject has a small waist), is effective. A seated position with a towel placed casually against the leg can give the illusion of the thighs being thinner. We're speaking here of cases where the face and upper body warrant the trouble of working around the lower body problems.

One word of advice when you are trying to copy a pose from a magazine or poster: remember that everyone is different and sometimes there is no such thing as duplicating *exactly* the twist and turns of one body when working with a different set of bones and muscle. If you see that it isn't working out, modify the pose to suit your model. Something even better might evolve.

When every part of the body has been posed to look its very best, then the face can be turned one way and then another to find the most pleasing angle.

Because models are generally tall, it follows that in most cases their feet are large. Subjects with beautifully shaped hands and feet are a real pleasure to photograph. But, if the feet are too big, flat, and large, I try to ameliorate the situation by hiding them in a natural manner: have the model sit on them, curl them around toward the background, and, if standing, have her high on her toes. I've designed an aid for this pose: a block of wood the shape of an instep. This, placed under one foot, gives the model an anchor so that she can balance better. A second aid to posing that I carry with me at all times is a set of soft foam rubber pads in an oval shape. I have one set in black and another that is covered with flesh-colored material. The black one can be placed in a stream, in the surf, or in the grass, and the knee can be situated on it instead of the ground to prevent pain and the chance of marking up the skin for other poses. The flesh-colored one is used when the knee cannot be hidden by water or whatever. If the pad shows slightly it can be easily retouched because it so closely resembles the skin tones.

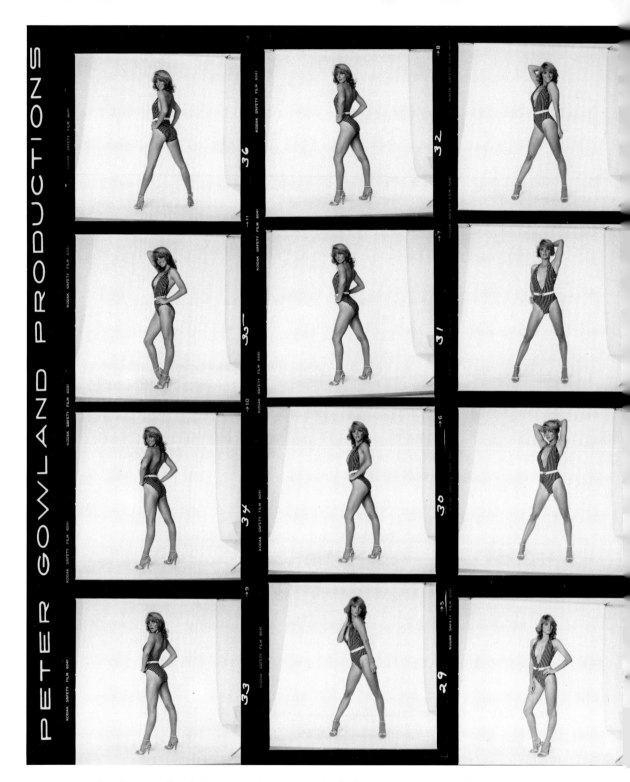

Proof sheet. Studio is set up for postery look. Here we wanted to feature model Karen Witter's legs; holding camera at waist level caused the least distortion to the body. From a variety of poses, we selected #28 and #35 as the best. Four Strobosol lights on background, key light at #2 position camera left.

By having the model stand with legs apart and hips twisted one is able to emphasize the waist-line and add curves to a typical poster pose. Camera was just below hip level, looking up on the face and down at the legs. Hasselblad with 80mm lens. Gowland Swing Light with Larson 72-inch Hex was at the #1 position, which creates the shadow gradation on the body. This is the type of lighting that pinup artists Vargas and Petty used. Four direct Strobosols evened out the background. *Model, Karen Witter.*

ANGLES

Don't be afraid to move around with your camera. Alice is a great one for this. I'll be photographing a model and she'll be studying the situation from a vantage point that is oblique to mine and quickly call me to see what I think. Some of my better pictures have resulted from just that sort of happening. It's important to know that there is more than one camera position, especially when working outdoors where background can interfere with your subject. Shooting down from a high angle eliminates confusing skylines or bushes and trees. Seating the model on a railing, with the camera at a low angle, gives a clear sky area. Moving around to the side or back creates a unique composition. Just don't take everything from the static, front placement of the camera, at waist level. Incidentally, waist level is the ideal camera height for taking photographs of a model standing—it provides the least amount of distortion.

When I take pictures from a high angle, I try to compose the subject in a diagonal line across the film, leaning back to become flat to the plane of the film. This helps eliminate the enlargement of feet or head and keeps the whole body in proper perspective.

When shooting from a low angle, I make sure that the feet are not closest to the camera, otherwise they increase by at least one size.

Another example of high and low camera angles (note the horizon). The rock, shot from two different angles, shows the two types of lighting: the first picture is backlighted by the sun; in the second, the sun is in a #4 position. Hasselblad with 80mm lens and Norman 200-B on camera. *Model, Holly Huddleston.*

With camera at horizon level, model Stephanie McLean extends leg and stands on the toes of both feet, with a twist to her hips, thus lengthening and slimming the lines of her body. Hasselblad with 80mm lens. Norman 200-B on camera in position #1 and the sun at #5 behind model.

This candid pose, caught while model was relaxing, makes an unusual composition. I've found that girls with slim legs can be made to appear heavier by photographing them from a rear angle. No auxiliary lights were used. Hasselblad with 80mm lens. *Model, Debra Gaske.*

An antique piano stool helps this pose of dancer Iris Rounsaville. Pentax camera with 55mm lens. Lighting was one hard quartz light at a #2 position (high). A second light was on the background.

A high stool makes an excellent posing prop to show off the long legs of model Alretha Baker. We used poster lighting of four Stro-bosols on background and one Gowland Swing Light with 72-inch Hex at the #2 position camera right.

At the beach one can find all manner of helpful things, such as this Hobie-Cat, which lent it-self to a seated pose. I prefer to have the sand clear of footprints and would have moved the boat had the owner been around. The sun is in the #5 position backlighting the model, while the Norman 200-B is in the #2 position off camera to the left. Hasselblad with 80mm lens. *Model, Georgette Welborn.*

This high angle features the body and face but should have been taken with a less cluttered background. In color, with the green foliage, there is more definition between the model and her surroundings. Hasselblad with 80mm lens. Sun was in #4 position left; Norman 200-B was on the camera. *Model, Jilanne Leigh.*

An excellent way to show the torso is to pose the model with one knee resting high on a flat table and the other leg disappearing behind her. The forward placement of the knee allows the curve of the buttocks to be emphasized and the waist to be diminished. Note that the hands are away from the body, careful not to interfere with the lines. Hasselblad with 80mm lens. One 880 Strobonar was placed behind the model's head; her body covered the stand. One Gowland Swing Light with Larson 72-inch Hex was used from a #1 position behind camera. *Model, Shelly Winnaman.*

Proof sheet of model Stacy Alden.

From a kneeling position one can place the camera at face level or above. Face level, in this case, brings in the background to clutter the area behind model Stacy Alden's head. By raising the camera level, Stacy's entire body and head stand out against a clear area. Sun is coming in from a #5 backlight position; the flash, a Norman 200-B, filled in from the #1 position on the camera. The Hasselblad with 80mm lens was used for black and white, while the Gowlandflex 4 x 5 with 180mm lens was used for 4 x 5 color transparencies.

Beauty contest winner Teresa Ring, Miss California, poses on knees with hips twisted slightly to her right. Picture would have been improved by a better background. Sun is in #4 position, Norman 200-B on camera in #1 position. Hasselblad with 80mm lens. Gowlandflex was used for the 4 x 5 color transparencies.

Beach setting with umbrella used as a colorful prop. In the first picture, camera is level with horizon, affording the maximum amount of blue sky to complement model's tan skin. One foot extended adds length to the body. In second picture, variation on same low angle features legs and curves of body. Lighting for both pictures was the sun at #5 position (high) behind model, with the Norman 200-B on the camera. In third picture, camera has gone around to the other side and the sun is now the sole source of light, coming from a #2 position camera left. This gives a clear sand background with a touch of white foam and a hat, used as a prop. Hasselblad for black-and-white negatives and Gowlandflex 4 x 5 for color. *Model, Caroline Stone.*

The sand takes on a smooth, un-cluttered look just after a wave has washed over it. If model is careful to tiptoe into position, it remains that way. A dancer, Jilanne Leigh uses her hands and legs in graceful positions. Sun was in the #5 position and the strobe was on the camera in the #1 position. Hasselblad for black and white, Gowlandflex for 4 x 5 color.

The camera is at cheek level, focusing attention on bosom and face. The wind is coming from one direction and the strobe from another. The strobe coming from the #2 position camera left creates dark shadows and emphasizes cleavage. This pose and lighting are helpful to models who are not as generously endowed. Hasselblad with 80mm lens for black and white, Gowlandflex for 4 x 5 color. *Model, Holly Huddleston.*

The pretzel pose, where both legs are folded, one behind the other, is usually shot from a high angle. This position may cause girls with thighs on the thin side to look heavier than they are. Jill Osborn, a gymnast, does not have that problem. This pose features the most body in the least amount of space. Personally, I would have preferred the sand around her to be smooth. Hassel-blad with 80mm lens. Sun was in the #4 position and the Norman 200-B, on the camera, was in the #1 position.

These two pictures illustrate the difference between a compressed pose and an extended pose. Both were taken with the same model at approximately the same time. I do not consider the first one to be a good photograph in any way. The second one stretches the model's body, and with toes pointed and different lighting she has not only become thinner but taller. Shawna Roebuck is 5 feet 2 inches, so this extended pose works in her favor. First photograph was taken with Hasselblad with Gowland Swing Light in a #2 position camera left, with four lights on background. The second was taken with window light and two 17-inch Larson translucent umbrellas through which a 200-watt-second Norman strobe was fired. The strobe was at the #2 position camera right. The exposure ratio was determined by first using the Polaroid as a test, which enabled us to see where the light was bouncing off the window and to move the strobe accordingly. Hasselblad with 80mm lens was used for both pictures.

Therese Hallquist poses for "before" picture in Gowland studio. In front of her is the Larson 72-inch Hex on the Gowland Swing Light. A mirror on wheels is at the spot where the camera will be placed. Top of picture shows Ascor boom light, approximately 100 watt-seconds, and the 880 Strobonar in back of model. Both the hair light and the background light are fired by "slaves," electronic sensors attached to the hair light and background light. They pick up the light from the key when it fires and causes the hair light and background light to fire simultaneously; sometimes called "strobe triggers." They are wireless and have male AC plugs.

8

CLOTHING, HAIR, MAKEUP

CLOTHING

In working with clothing, one has a different challenge than that presented by straight glamour. The model, for one thing, must look good in the garments. Generally, the taller girls (5 feet 8 inches to 5 feet 10 inches) are best suited. While it's a bonus to find a girl with perfect features, the allover look and style of the model is what counts in fashion photography. We select someone who has a flare for posing, whose hair lends itself to easy and quick changes of style.

I've learned to thoroughly question clients about how they perceive the finished result and in that way I avoid expending energy, money, and time on something that turns out to be not at all what they had in mind. A local women's boutique employed my services to photograph their line of clothing for a black-and-white brochure. After looking over their fashions, the majority in pastels and summery colors, I suggested a neutral gray background because it would complement both the light and dark tones. A white background would not have separated the lighter materials and a black background would have interfered with the darker areas.

The model, a friend of the client, was a very pretty girl of only about 5 feet 6 inches but she managed to carry off the sitting very well because she was evenly proportioned and gave the impression of being taller than she actually was.

I keep my camera at waist level when photographing full-length fashion or glamour. This causes the least amount of distortion to the figure and the clothing. For drama and texture I elected to use #3 (side-light) lighting on most of the pictures. I was careful to have the model turn her head in the direction of the light so that it would not be cross-lit along with the garments.

Clothing photographed against a plain background can be spiced up with movement by the model or by the use of props: a chair, a hat, a parasol. Alice makes sure that we always have a supply of miscellaneous feminine accoutrements handy and clients can often supply scarfs, jewelry, or even something from their window display. All these help in making the photographs something special. On the more complicated catalog jobs, an additional stylist is usually hired to take care of these added touches.

Occasionally we work with two or three models at one time. This decreases the percentage of printable pictures in which all subjects look good at once, but by taking enough exposures we improve the chances. Also, I am careful to select people who have worked with others rather than choose new faces to the modeling scene. I've found that one extrovert can help the others and usually these group pictures are more fun. When I work with two or more subjects I use a different lighting arrangement because the #3 lighting, while excellent for one subject, may block the light from hitting the others. I frequently use a "ring" system (I built it myself, see page 141) whereby my lens extends through a box that contains one bare flash tube. With this, there are no readily discernible shadows in the finished picture.

The light literally surrounds the model. It is excellent for eliminating wrinkles in clothing and in people. Another advantage is that one can move freely about from room to room carrying the camera, either on a tripod or not, with the strobe-pack slung over the shoulder. The disadvantage is that in moving closer to or farther from the subject, one must change exposure to compensate for the difference in flash distances. I have taped a chart of these values to the ring light.

Photographing clothing outdoors gives the photographer a wide-open field. He can photograph with almost any kind of lighting, including that terrible midday sun, and the backgrounds do not necessarily have to relate realistically to the garment. I'm thinking of the lingerie catalogs and ads that show models in lacy teddies by a swimming pool or in a garden rather than in a bedroom setting, or evening wear against the sand and surf. Finding clear areas of wood, stucco, or brick with interesting side areas to complement the setting is not always easy; but, on the other hand, it isn't always necessary to show the entire figure, and thus porches, walkways, and gates can be utilized without detracting from the clothes. Gardens with backlighting can work because the green, if not lit heavily by sun, becomes a black area to work against and the model can be separated from the background by sun-backlighting her. If you envy those photographers who go for a week at a time to some resort hotel, remember that the pace is fast and there isn't much time to relax and enjoy the scenery. With fashion, the hours are all day, changing clothes quickly, thinking of new groupings and areas, moving reflectors and lights. Naturally there are assistants, but in the end the hundreds of pictures are edited down to just a few. These jobs are usually reserved for those who have been in the business long enough to have proven themselves to be good business persons in addition to having artistic talent. They have learned to work well with art directors who like to think of themselves as the directors, which they are. The jobs available to beginners are with local shops or designers who are willing to take a chance with an unknown because they haven't generated the income and fame to hire the well-known fashion names. This can be good for both parties: the photographer can add to his portfolio and have greater freedom in his selection of techniques, and the client keeps within the budget.

HAIR AND MAKEUP

Women's hairstyles change constantly and I'm convinced it is only because those involved in the world of beauty feel the necessity to be different, otherwise why would anyone put a perm in shiny, straight hair or change black hair to blond? The old saying "woman's hair is her crowning glory" is hard to believe with today's wild assortment of colors and lengths, usually never combed! For this reason I am elated when I find a woman who has said no to popular fads and sits before my camera with healthy, shiny, well-groomed tresses. I find that hairstylists can help when I'm faced with someone who has problem hair—either too fine or too thick—and the fee paid is worth it.

My clients who buy the look of the subject rather than that of the clothing still prefer long hair, at least to the shoulders, with as little styling as possible. They prefer the natural look. For this reason my stock photo file requires pictures that are not readily dated. I can think of two pictures, taken over thirty years ago, where the model's subtle makeup and windblown hair give the impression that they are recent photos. It is only the clothing that places them in a certain period in time.

 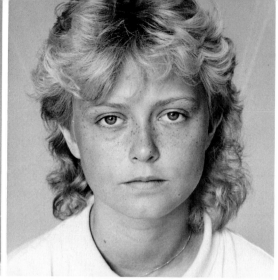

"Before" pictures show that freckles are a part of Therese Hallquist's natural charm, but we wanted to cover them to give her a more glamorous appearance. Here, she wears no makeup whatsoever.

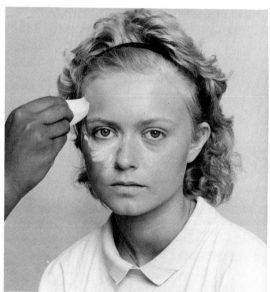 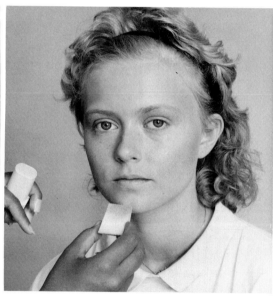

Step 1. Makeup artist Analeese Aran first applies a white cream called a "concealer." This is a professional product and should not be confused with the "clown white" makeup. The tone, while appearing as white, is actually tinted with a slight mint hue that helps to eliminate red or brown areas on the skin. It is applied to freckles and would be applied under the eyes to dark circles if Therese had them. In the past, before I knew better, several of my models used a pure white product, and even though they covered it with a natural base the flash penetrated the base and the white showed under the eyes in the finished pictures.

Steps 2 and 3. A shade of Max Factor Pan-stik is applied all over the face and neck area. Notice how freckles are disappearing. A darker shade of the Pan-stik is applied to the cheeks to give slight shading. A lighter touch is applied to the cheekbones.

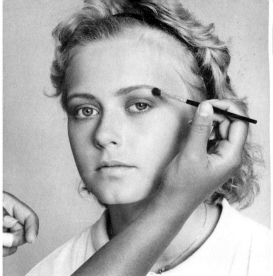

Step 4. Eye shadow, in the form of powder, is applied with a brush. We prefer the browns and plum tones for a more natural look. A lighter shade is applied to the upper lid, just below eyebrow. Eyebrows are lightly accentuated with brown pencil.

Step 5. First, lipstick pencil is used to very lightly outline the lips. This is blended into the rest of the lips by using a brush and additional lipstick if needed. Last, mascara is applied to the eyelashes, and the corners of the eyes are very gently emphasized by liner that fades as it progresses to inner corner.

Finished makeup. A pretty, young face that looks completely natural. Photo was made by using the Larson 72-inch Hex on the Gowland Swing Light at a #2 position to add slight shading to the face. Below the chin, between model and camera, a Vari-Flector by Smith-Victor was placed on a stand in a flat position to bounce the key light from this low angle. Note the double key lights in eyes. There was one light on the background, and the Ascor boom light lighted the hair from above. Hasselblad with 150mm lens; #3 Harrison & Harrison diffusion filter. *Model, Therese Hallquist.*

Amie Johnson with no makeup and hair that has been permed.

Amie, after makeup and hairstyling. Hair was put in hot rollers to make a softer curl. Gowland Swing Light coming from #2 position camera left, with the Smith-Victor Vari-Flector placed below model's chin between camera and model. No hair light was used.

Hair must be freshly shampooed! Seems obvious but I'm surprised at some professional models who come to the sitting with dull hair, rolled in curlers, hoping to cover up the need for washing. They are ushered immediately into the shower.

I do not hire a makeup artist for every sitting—only when I see that the subject needs help. For the most part, the models I use have learned to apply makeup neatly and sparingly, but for those who over- or underdo it, I have an excellent person who has consistently proven her skill—Analeese Aran. She seems to understand what I want and has a talent for knowing just how to bring out the best in a model's features without having the makeup look obvious. Other makeup artists whom I've tried can't seem to control the urge to "paint" the face.

Because I've been in the glamour business for so many years, I've seen makeup trends come and go and I'm happy to note that the latest theme is the "un-made-up" look. That means the makeup used does not show, but *it is there!*

Preparing for picture of Amie Johnson and Therese Hallquist, Alice Gowland does a last-minute touch-up on Therese's hair.

This is an example of shadowless lighting made possible with "homemade" ring light. Ordinarily there would be shadows on the background because the models are placed against it, leaving no room for additional lights. Excellent setup when working with two people together. Hasselblad with 80mm lens and Norman 800-watt-second power pack with an Ascor flash tube next to the lens. *Models, Amie Johnson and Therese Hallquist.*

Amie Johnson and Therese Hall-quist in portrait pose made with the Gowland ring light, which casts just the slightest shadow under the chin. Hasselblad with 150mm lens was used to avoid distortion on close-up.

These five pictures, taken against a gray background, were shot for Whispers, a local boutique. The Gowland Swing Light, with the 72-inch Larson Hex, was placed in the #2 position camera left. With the aid of a mirror next to the camera, model Nadine Reimers was able to position herself with little direction. Hasselblad with 80mm lens.

When we pivoted the Swing Light to the opposite side, to almost the #3 position, we asked Nadine to face the light, with her body front, so the resulting shadows would add detail to the white jacket. Hasselblad with 80mm lens.

While we were shooting full-length pictures of model Nadine Reimers, our hairdresser suggested this windswept look for the hair which would focus attention on the hat. Hasselblad with 150mm lens; Gowland Swing Light in #2 left position. *Hairdresser, Marice Irwin, of Michel Michele International, Pacific Palisades.*

To show off this casual summer dress, we selected our favorite background—the beach. Sun was in the #5 position, but high. Total lighting for the front was the Norman 200-B on the camera, in the #1 position. Hasselblad with 80mm lens. *Model, Georgette Welborn.*

Wanting to demonstrate the effect of harsh sunlight on black clothing, which requires brilliance to show off detail, Mary Lee Gowland posed against the stark white wall and turned her face to the sun. Pentax camera with 55mm macro lens.

Although in a clear area, without benefit of additional light the action of the model's head could not be stopped by the shutter speed chosen by the camera's automatic mechanism. With the model in the shade, the sun behind her, the camera selected the slower shutter speed. Had a wider f/stop been used, the camera would automatically have selected a faster speed. The lens used was 85mm, on the Pentax ME, which does not have the manual shutter feature. *Model, Mary Lee Gowland.*

An ideal garden location is one where model will receive hair light from the sun in a #4, back, position and the areas behind her are dark so they do not conflict with the clothing. We also look for some type of prop to help the model in posing, in this case a fence. Front light was a Norman 200-B on the camera, which was a Hasselblad with 80mm lens. *Model, Kerry Fotre.*

Plain background was used to accentuate the classic lines of this silk lounging outfit. Alretha Baker, a dancer as well as a model, posed easily. A Gowland Swing Light with a 72-inch Larson Hex was at the #2 camera right position; a hair light from above made a highlight on her arm. Hasselblad with 80mm lens.

Sports designs are often shown by two models so the advertiser can get two garments into the same picture. Two models also create an opportunity for action and a more natural look. Here I used my homemade ring light in order to eliminate shadows. Because the bulb is an 800-watt-second it has the advantage over the smaller-powered ring lights on the market. The larger the film size, the smaller the f/ stop and the more power needed. Hasselblad with 80mm lens. Color was also taken with the Hasselblad. *Models, Alretha Baker and Francesca.*

Working with mime Anita Ashley, who does her own makeup, provided us with a file of stock photos on the subject. Gowland Swing Light in #2 position with four lights on background. Hasselblad with 150mm lens.

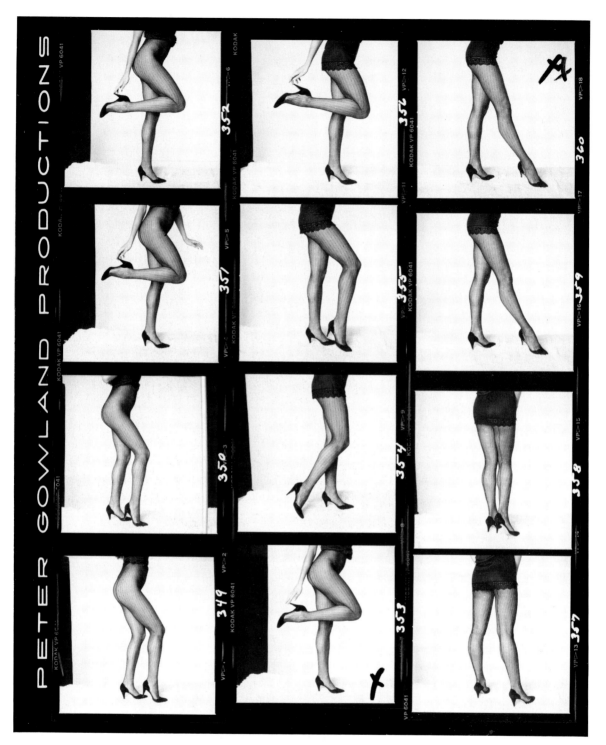

Proof sheet of model Shelly Winnaman. We used a white background to set off the net stockings. Out of this group we selected 360, 353, and 354. By trying every angle we found that it was easy to see how *not* to pose legs. However, it was interesting to note that had our model had skinny legs, poses similar to those in 357 and 358—from the back, emphasizing the calves and thighs— would have made them appear heavier. The model stood on a low table with a carpet over it so we could get light behind her. We had two Strobosols on either side, hitting the background, with one main light, the Gowland Swing Light in the #1 position. Hasselblad with 80mm lens.

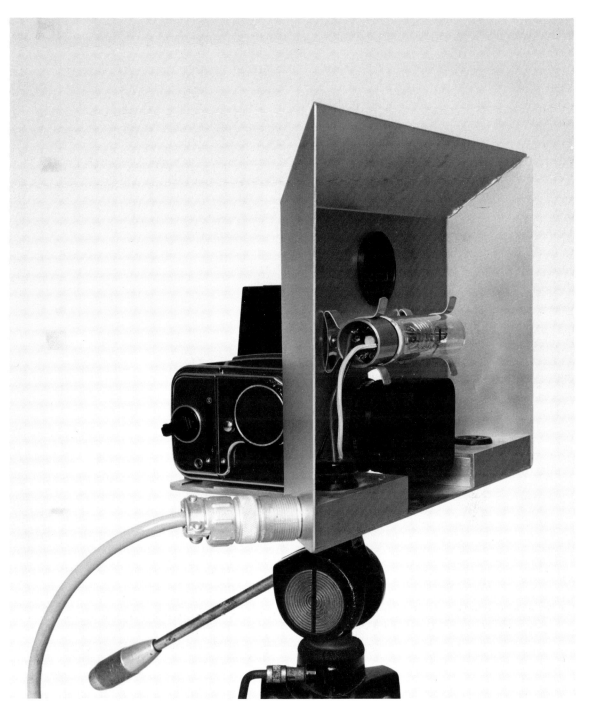

Ring light. I made this aluminum box with two holes (top hole is used with the Gowlandflex). The lens shade protects the lens from the flash tube that is directly above it. Wiring runs into a plug that is connected to a Norman 800-watt-second unit.

Having the model lie down on a low table covered with black felt and photographing her against a black background makes her legs appear slimmer. The Gowland Swing Light from the #1 position was the front light. At the #4 position, from 3/4 rear, four Strobosols were turned toward the model's legs. In the 8 x 10 prints we had an artist black out the highlights on the wrinkles in the black material. We selected 380 and 382 from the proof sheet. Hasselblad with 80mm lens. *Model, Shelly Winnaman.*

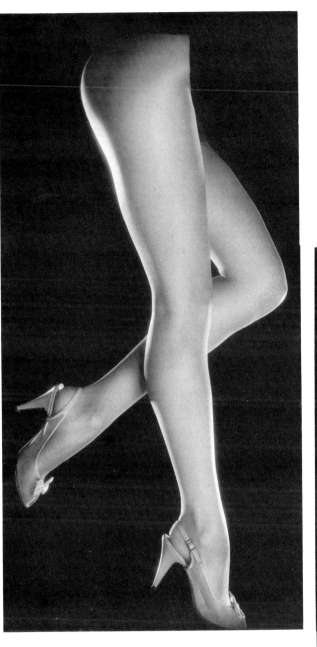
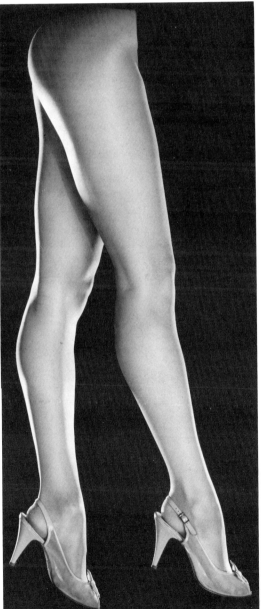

Outdoor portrait using the sun for backlighting and a Norman 200-B strobe for the front. Hasselblad with 150mm Sonnar lens. Model Stephanie Drake holds a flower as a whimsical bit of business to go along with the setting.

9

THE ROLE
OF THE PROP

The picture that comes to mind when I think of "props" is the famous Richard Avedon credit taken of Nastassia Kinski with the boa constrictor. Here's a case where the subject is famous and didn't have to agree to posing with a snake but probably did so willingly because she was aware of the photographer's impeccable reputation. I don't know how that particular photograph came about but it piqued my interest not only because of its originality and exquisite composition, but because I, too, had worked with a model and her pet snake. While the results of my sitting were different in lighting and composition, being all black and white, it was the snake that made the distinction between an ordinary picture and one that attracts instant attention.

Props can help the imagination. The example cited may be extreme but it illustrates the importance of being alert to objects that can add a new dimension to your pictures.

In my own experience I've found it invaluable to make note of interesting pieces of furniture or objets d'art whether they are in an antique store or at the home of a friend. I may think about them for a while before actually putting them to use and have, on occasion, photographed a chair or a vase or an old picture frame alone with the idea of using it later either as a second exposure to a nude study or superimposing one positive on another (when a color slide is involved).

THE ON-SIGHT PROP

When photographing on location one should search for areas where there are man-made objects, such as boats, fences, and stairways, or nature's offerings, such as rock formations, logs, driftwood, trees. I'm a stickler for plain backgrounds, but I find that the introduction of another element into a photograph of a pretty girl leads to a wide variety of poses and compositions. Rocks, for example, when found near the surf act as a support for sitting or leaning and also cause the waves to fan out in exciting splash formations, each one unique. Be careful that the rock is in the right place, and don't use it just because it's there. By right place I mean in relation to the sun. I prefer the sun in back of the model or to the side, since it gives a nice, bright edge-light to her body and does not cause her to squint. I use flash to light her. So, if the rock is situated in such a way that she is forced to face the sun, either she has to close her eyes, as though sunbathing, or look most uncomfortable.

In lieu of a rock in the surf, I have sometimes found large pieces of driftwood that serve the same purpose. When working in parks it's best to find clear spaces, using trees as an edge rather than as a background. Sometimes benches are situated on slight rises so the public can sit and enjoy an elevated view and these make excellent locations for a group of poses.

THE PORTABLE PROP

Whether I am going to a different interior background or outdoor location, I take along what I call "standard" props for glamour pictures: a hat, a colorful towel, sunglasses, an antique mirror, pearls, feathers, or any other object that has a feminine look. Pearls, particularly, lend a touch of class. I know they've been used extensively in both advertising and in the men's magazines, but they're such a great standby when there's a lull or both model and photographer have run dry on the creative end. Give her a string of pearls and see what happens!

Chairs with interesting designs combine beautifully with women. But they should be unusual—not just the ordinary kitchen or dining chair—usually on the delicate side rather than overstuffed and cumbersome. I've taken chairs to the beach or used them in the studio against a plain background—or set them in the woods.

Boats may not seem portable, but I've discovered that since only a section of a boat is necessary to get the idea across, I've included in my supply of portable props the tip of a catamaran. It's about 6 feet in length and fits into my car. We can carry it down to the edge of the surf or settle it in the dry sand, and the model can either sit on it or stand next to it. The finished picture gives the impression that she's seated on the real thing.

THE ACCIDENTAL PROP

I never know what the finished picture is going to look like even though I have made preparations as to background, costume, and so on, because there is always the unexpected. What comes to mind is a day at Malibu beach, working with Georgette Welborn. I had posed her on a particular rock, one backlit, when a man walked by with a green parrot on his shoulder. Georgette was wearing a bikini that was almost the same color green. We asked if the bird was friendly and, when told that it was, we asked if Georgette could hold it for a picture. She did, and the bird really gave the photograph the touch that was needed to set it apart from the everyday pinup.

I've been disappointed in some objects that I've used. A ladder, for example, that was made of metal and had no sense of design other than for utility spoiled an otherwise nice pose. A rusty chain-link fence near the surf, part of a jetty, looked at first to have interesting texture and form but in the finished picture it was just a bit too rough next to the pretty model. So one has to learn to be particular. The prop should embellish the picture and not take away from the beauty of the model.

Here a beach ball was brought along for both color and posing. *Model, Caroline Stone.*

A piece of kelp found floating near shore made a good prop for model Stephanie McLean.

Since the foam acts as a reflector, we cut the exposure from f/11 to f/16. Striped towel adds color and action and assists model in posing. *Model, Nancy Fletcher.*

These three pictures were taken around midday with the Hasselblad, using the 80mm lens, a Norman 200-B strobe, and Verichrome pan film. Exposure was 1/500 second at f/11 with the strobe 8 feet from the model.

Wet suit and accompanying fins allowed for a casual and unconventional pose that looks perfectly natural for model Shelly Winnaman. Norman 200-B strobe was the source of light here; only a small patch of sun hit her knee. Hasselblad with 80mm lens, Verichrome pan film, and yellow-green filter to darken the sky and protect the lens from ocean spray. Exposure was 1/250 second at f/11, which was one-stop open for the filter factor of 2x (2 times).

We photographed model Teresa Ring late in the day with the sun as the only source of light and the foam acting as a reflector. Wind catching the towel makes a pleasing composition. Taken with Hasselblad, using 80mm lens and Verichrome pan film. Exposure was 1/500 second at f/11.

Surf mat of bright red gives Suzee Slater a soft surface for her knee to rest on. Red props lend a warm color to the overall blue of the ocean background. Hasselblad with 80mm lens. Exposure was 1/500 second at f/11 with yellow-green filter and Norman 200-B strobe at 8 feet.

A unique-looking wicker chair brought along to the beach and placed in the most unlikely area of the surf allows for a variety of poses not usually feasible without the use of a chair. Hasselblad with 80mm lens, Verichrome pan film. Exposure was f/11 at 1/500 second, with yellow-green filter. I use the faster shutter speed when the surf is foamy and white to allow for detail in that area of the photo. *Model, Georgette Welborn.*

Finding an interesting location at the beach where a freshwater stream goes into the ocean, we were able to take advantage of the sun sparkling on the water. Exposure was f/12 with a Norman 200-B strobe on the Gowlandflex 4 × 5 camera; Kodak Ektachrome film ASA 64. *Model, Kerry Fotre.*

Western theme suggested by swinging doors and dark background with five backlights—one at the top and two at either side in the #4 position. Front light was a 100-watt-second Strobonar 880. Gowlandflex camera with 210mm Symmar lens and Kodak Ektachrome ASA 64 film. *Model, Linda Gordeuk.*

In order to give more curves to the body in a standing pose, we supported a flat piece of wood between two sawhorses and covered it with Mylar. Shelly Winnaman, the model, was able to put her weight on the back left leg, place her right leg on top of the Mylar gently, and give a twist to her body. Key light was the Gowland Swing Light at position #1. Strobonar 880 behind her head position #5 and two Strobosols at 45 degrees behind at position #4 (one on each side). Red cellophane was placed over backlights, giving colorful edge light to her figure and hair.

Usually there is not much color at the beach, and that mainly blue or white, so we try to add a bit of color with a towel or other prop. We used the Norman 200-B strobe on the camera, in the #1 position. Gowlandflex with 210mm lens and Kodak Ektachrome film. Exposure was 1/400 second at f/12. *Model, Nancy Fletcher.*

Green foliage is difficult to photograph because it absorbs light at a greater rate than other colors, so I generally overexpose it by about two stops and have the model illuminated by strobe with the sun behind her. This way we can use the shutter speed to control the amount of light on the background. The f/stop controls the amount of light from the strobe, which in this case was the Norman 200-B in the #1 position, front. Gowlandflex with 210mm Symmar lens. *Model, Caroline Bartlett.*

When not working on assignment and planning to use the photographs to expand our stock photo file, we frequently use seasonal themes such as here for Valentine's Day. This increases chances of sales for advertising or calendars. Model is Audrey Bradshaw using key light in #1 position. Gowlandflex camera, 4 × 5 Fujichrome film.

Taking advantage of a Hobie-Cat (catamaran) beached between runs. Noonday sun with the Norman 200-B strobe on the camera, in the #1 position. Gowlandflex 4 × 5 twin-lens camera with Fujichrome film. *Model, Georgette Welborn.*

Tra-C DiPonzio, dancer-actress, leaped into water spray thrown from each side in this outdoor, night shot. Action was rehearsed for prefocus and composition. Gowlandflex with 180mm lens was on tripod. Polaroids showed timing was best when water was thrown slightly before Tra-C's leap. Key light at #2 position was a Norman 800-watt strobe. Four Strobosols at #4 position. Go-bos blocked backlights. All lights at 10 feet from subject. Thirty-six exposures were made at 1/500th, f/11 on 4 × 5 Fujichrome ASA 100.

Creating a feminine atmosphere with lace curtains and a lace garment. Two 36-inch Larson translucents in the #2 position camera right were lighted with two Larson Strobosols. One additional light, a Honeywell 880 Strobonar, hit the background at camera left. Gowlandflex with 180mm lens, Fujichrome film. *Model, Linda Johnson.*

Using the curved trunk of a sycamore tree, model Valerie Ojala poses in a sylvan setting. A reflector was held by an assistant at the #4 position camera right in an attempt to separate Valerie from the foliage behind her. A Norman 200-B strobe was used on the camera in the #1 position. Hasselblad with 80mm lens.

I prefer to photograph brunettes against a dark background because I can use more light on their hair, which takes more light than you would think. Beads used as a prop help the model with facial expression and add action to the scene. Key light was the Gowland Swing Light with the Larson 72-inch Hex in the #1 position. Two Larson Strobosols were used to light the hair from the #4 position. Hasselblad, 150mm lens. *Model, Alretha Baker.*

Trellis with ivy makes a nice frame for Caroline Stone's beautiful face and figure. Subject was backlighted by the sun in the #4 position right and lighted from the front by a Norman 200-B in the #1 position, on the camera. Gowlandflex and Fujichrome ASA 100 film.

At a parking lot in Malibu, sour grass flowers were growing along the edge and down the bank to the sand. By putting a towel down and taking the picture from a low angle, with the sand and sea in the background, we can hide from you the fact that Teresa Ring is only a few inches away from the asphalt. The sun was at the #4 position camera right and the Norman 200-B was mounted on the camera, in the #1 position. Gowlandflex with 210 Symmar lens and 4 × 5 Fujichrome film. Picture was shot horizontally because calendar companies want the option of printing vertically as well.

Overcast day provides soft lighting to the background, while the model is lighted by a Norman 200-B on the camera, in the #1 position. This pose is typical of those preferred by calendar companies. Model Michelle Hansen's young, fresh look, combined with the colorful flowers, makes the picture salable. Gowlandflex with 210mm Symmar lens and Fujichrome film. If I had wanted to get closer I would have used a 240mm or 300mm lens on the 4 × 5 camera.

A gimmicky stock photo theme, with black background. The key light was a 36-inch Larson Soff Box powered by an 800-watt-second Norman strobe; it was placed on the floor in front of the model. A piece of yellow tissue paper was placed over the Soff Box to produce a warm, firelike quality. We used a hair light above and two Strobosols at the #4 positions, one on either side. Gowlandflex with Ektachrome ASA 64 film. *Model, Camilla Kay.*

Hilltop with a fence provides a nice setting for Teresa Ring. The day was overcast, so by underexposing the white sky by using a faster shutter speed, we darkened it slightly. Teresa is the type of model we look for: beautiful complexion, features, hair, and a lovely smile. Norman 200-B strobe at the #1 position, on the camera. Gowlandflex with 210mm lens on 4 × 5 Fujichrome ASA 100 film.

By finding a tree on a bluff we were able to use its trunk as a leaning post and the sea and grass as the background. This was taken late in the day with the sun in the #4 position camera right and the Norman 200-B strobe in the #1 position, on the camera. *Model, Nancy Fletcher.*

A high angle gives us a clear sand background and easy positioning of legs. No strobe was necessary here because the angle put the sun in the key light position, #1 above the camera, which is nice for body shadows but means that the model must close her eyes or look away. I held the Hasselblad over my head and viewed the groundglass by looking up into it. *Model, Alretha Baker.*

A blue-and-white golf umbrella gives Caroline Stone something to lean on and provides an additional touch of color. Notice that the sand is free of footprints. An advantage of working in an area where the surf comes up is that the water erases footprints on the sand. Hasselblad with 80mm lens, Verichrome pan film. Exposure was 1/250 second at f/11.

Sometimes you come upon a catamaran or some other piece of water equipment, as in this case with model Stephanie Drake. We used only the prow so it would not dominate the scene. Picture would have been improved by moving the boat closer to the water and eliminating the footprints in the background. Hasselblad with 80mm lens, Verichrome pan film. Exposure was 1/250 second at f/11, with Norman 200-B attached to the camera.

When a model has nothing to work with, or gets hungry, she can munch on her hair! Here we are using a 150mm Sonnar lens on the Hasselblad and shooting out into the bright surf using a Norman 200-B strobe. We purposely over-exposed the background and shot at 1/125 second at f/11 with Verichrome pan film. *Model, Suzee Slater.*

Assistants, Dean Cuadra on the right and Kahn on the left, control the added elements to the "Eve in the Garden" setup constructed in the patio. By using a 6-by-6-foot frame covered with black felt, the background becomes a solid area against which the fern fronds stand out. *Model, Bettina.*

On location in Jenner, California, model Shawn Harb is caught wheeling her barrow across the property, creating a satirical composition. Actually, Shawn was clothed when I first saw her carting some leaves, and it just seemed like a humorous idea. Pentax camera, 50mm lens, T-Max film. Exposure was 1/250 second at f/8. No flash fill.

Portrait of a secretary, and what better props than glasses and a pencil—they tell it all. Taken with the Hasselblad, using 150mm Sonnar lens in the studio with one Honeywell 100-watt-second strobe behind model's hair and directed at the camera, with a main light, a 6-foot Larson Super Silver Hex at 45-degree #2 position camera right. No other lights were used. *Model, Margaret Shumar.*

Model Linda Johnson holds pearls to give her hands something to do in this portrait taken against a window in our studio. One hair light (Ascor strobe) was used and four Larson 36-inch translucents (two on either side of the camera lens) with four Larson Strobosol electronic flash units. Notice the four catch-lights in the model's eyes. The lights were placed 72 inches from the model, and the exposure was f/16 with 1/8-second shutter speed to pick up the window light. Film was Verichrome pan (ASA 125).

Commercial setting which appeared as a color cover for a trade journal for the month of January uses balloons and streamers to suggest the season. Same photo was taken in color, but this one used Verichrome pan film at 1/125 second at f/16 with a Larson 72-inch Super Silver Hex placed at a #2 position about 8 feet from model at camera left. Additional strobes were used to light the background. *Model, Angela Nyseth.*

Calendar or poster setting using a replica of an authentic fast-draw gun combined with the cowboy chaps and hat may be on the corny side but sells well, especially when posed with Gina Gold. Hasselblad using 80mm lens. Two lights were placed at the #4 position, one on either side of model, with a fill light in the #1 position.

Cap pistols, looking very real, and a mean look from Sara Munson, make very little sense as far as reality is concerned but create a fantasy of "Pistol-Packin' Mama" for those who like guns and women. Hasselblad with 80mm lens, Verichrome pan film. Key light is a Larson 72-inch Hex Super Silver reflector at the #2 position camera right. This gives a roundness to the figure. Two Larson Strobosols were used on the background from camera left.

A pillow complements the costume here, but by using a white slip on the pillow, the picture becomes high key with the model standing out against the light background. Lights used were the 72-inch Larson Reflectasol from the #1, front, position with four lights directed at the background. *Model, Melissa Prophet.*

A towel, used with a wet model, makes sense. This picture was taken in the patio with a black felt background and sunlight coming from a #4 position. Reflector was used on the left side, also from the #4 position, and an electronic flash near the camera, from the #1 position. Front light was 50 percent less than the intensity of the sun. *Model, Bettina.*

Debra Gaske finds the circular stairway lends itself to natural poses with unlimited variations. No artificial lights were used, only the window light.

Here, direct sunlight from a #5 position silhouettes the model but highlights the string of pearls. Pearls are a natural prop for feminine subjects. *Model, Heather Haines.*

With lingerie as the costume, model employs an etched-glass bottle to give action to her hands. *Model, Shelly Winnaman.*

For this shot I connected a hair blower to a hose and used it like a vacuum cleaner in reverse. It was easier to direct than an ordinary electric fan, which has too wide a spread for this purpose. Placing a bare bulb light behind model Karen Stride, who is a brunette, caused her hair to appear white and to fan out like a peacock. The black background is important so that the hair can be seen clearly. The bare bulb behind Karen takes the #5 position, and the Gowland Swing Light with the 72-inch Larson Hex is in the #1 position. Hasselblad with 80mm lens.

10

S P E C I A L
E F F E C T S

One way to add some spice and interest to your glamour photography is with special effects.

FILTER AND DIFFUSION

You can soften your glamour portraits with either gauze (black netting) or a glass diffusion filter over the lens. With glass you don't have to increase the exposure; with gauze you do. Usually one-half stop is enough.

Remember, to get the full effect of a diffusion filter, one must see backlight. The amount of diffusing is related to the diffusion number on the filter as well as the focal length of the lens and the degree of f/stop. In other words, filters create greater diffusion with wide-open lenses. Stopping down the iris diaphragm will tend to neutralize the effect, making the picture sharper. I suggest that you make a series of tests with various diffusing filters with your lenses at different f/stops. Harrison & Harrison makes a series of black-dot glass filters with five different degrees of diffusion. They are sold only by the set and come in a hardwood box. I have found that they don't seem to cut down the contrast of the negatives as standard and star filters do, which can be an asset because most negatives taken with diffusion filters require an extra-hard grade of printing paper.

STAR FILTERS

If you are not familiar with star filters, try recalling a beauty pageant on television when the camera picked up the stage with all the lights showing above. The star filter makes streaks of light going in many directions. The number of directions will depend on the pattern of the lines on the filter itself, usually a four-point star.

DIFFUSION WHEN PRINTING

It is possible to add diffusion when printing by placing a filter under the lens at the time of exposure in the darkroom. I do this occasionally when the negative cannot be retouched or the retouching is too apparent. This softens the final result. Any kind of diffusion can be used, even cellophane. Instead of a total exposure with the filter, it can be used for part of the exposure. Experimenting will give you a choice. The advantage of diffusion in the printing, rather than when taking the picture, is that you have a choice of using a sharp picture or diffusing it. Whereas, if you diffuse in the camera, the negative is permanently diffused. Another consideration is that when diffusion is done in the camera, the highlights are spreading into the shadows, but this is reversed when diffusion is done in the darkroom, thus dulling the highlights.

EXCESSIVE GRAIN

Here again, I feel it is better to go-for-the-grain on the original negative. On one particular assignment, the art director wanted excessive grain. I had read that Kodak recording film 2475, ASA 1000, if pushed to 3200 ASA by using a meter setting of 3200 and developing the film for 8 minutes in DK-50 at 68 °F, would give a more pronounced grain.

I found that bleaching the negative in Kodak chromium intensifier, then redeveloping it in D-72 paper developer would increase the grainy effect.

TEXTURE SCREENS

When printing in the darkroom you can create the look of a painting or a graphic arts impression in the final picture by using texture screens over the projected image before development. These screens are sheets of plastic in which various patterns have been implanted.

1. Place a negative in the holder and make a test exposure using a small strip of printing paper.
2. Now place an 8 x 10 (or larger) sheet of paper in the easel and make the correct exposure. Do not remove the paper after doing this.
3. Place your choice of texture screen over the print and re-expose the same sheet of paper.

You may have to make several tests to see which degree of texture you prefer. The results that I like were achieved by putting the screen about one-quarter inch above the paper rather than directly on it. I printed the screen for the same amount of time allowed for the original print. Screens, when used with period costumes, can give an antique quality to the picture. Ask at your local camera store or art shop to find where these screens are available. Occasionally I've seen them advertised in photographic magazines. Normal negatives can be used, or copy negatives made from Kodalith Ortho Type Three #2556.

KODALITH NEGATIVES

I have had good luck making these Kodalith copy negatives from normal or soft prints. When you have a gray, flat-looking print of a very good subject, copy it on Kodalith, graphic arts film. This gives you an extremely high contrast negative where the grays become black and gray-looking whites become brilliant white. It is surprisingly easy. I use 4 x 5 sheet film but understand that on special order it can be purchased in 35mm format. Exposure is relatively long. I figure it at an ASA 8. My exposure is 1 second at f/14 with two 600-watt quartz lights at half power 20 inches from copy. I suggest you make a test with your own lights. The ASA 8 could be a starting point. There is very little latitude in the film. You must be right on or the negative will block up (lose your fine lines). I develop 3 minutes in D-72 paper developer much the same as making a black-and-white print.

FANS AND SCREENS

Strong electric fans, aimed at the hair, have become popular with Hollywood glamour portraitists. I'm not that happy about using them in the studio because the hair doesn't always fan out in a symmetrical pattern—and may block up in clumps. It's the factor of chance again, much as photographing your model running on the beach. You have to take many exposures and hope that one comes out just right. The action does give a portrait something special. I've found that when working near the studio, but outdoors, the fan works really well on days when the air is still. The outdoor background makes the action of the fan appear more realisitic than it does against the solid colors of a studio background. In fashion the fan works well, giving a billowy effect to skirts. For one assignment, of a girl with her skirt blowing up showing her legs much like the famous Marilyn Monroe picture, I did some improvising. In my junk closet I had an old device used to force hot air into a bathtub (somewhat like a Jacuzzi). I also had a prop chimney that we'd used on a previous assignment. The device was put inside the chimney and the air blew up through the vent. Artwork was necessary to block out the chimney, but the effect was great. We even sent in some autumn leaves to swirl around.

FLOOR REFLECTIONS

The floor in my studio is made of terrazzo and in most of the studio pictures I use paper rolls or carpeting to cover it. However, I frequently thought about the reflective quality that it has uncovered, particularly after it has been buffed by the cleaning service. In one of my experimental moods, when photographing a model named Bettina and her pet snake, "Buddy," I poured a small amount of water over the floor and asked her to lie down and assume some kind of pose with the snake as part of it. I must say she was a good sport because the warm water soon became cold and the hard surface wasn't very comfortable, yet she could see the exciting results in the mirror and so continued to pose for an hour or so. This was in the evening because my studio is daylight and I needed the darkness for the best results. The water would not have been a problem if I had been careful to alert my assistant (who kept pouring more on) to the possibility of it running into the dressing room, which it did. Had we paid closer attention we could have swept it into a nearby planter.

MYLAR FOR REFLECTIONS

In lieu of a terrazzo floor, silver or gold Mylar provides an excellent reflective surface. I buy it locally, by the yard, and keep it rolled on a cardboard tube. The Mylar doesn't give the true effect of water, and because it comes in 54-inch widths only, there is usually a seam where the two pieces join. One length usually isn't enough. I just lay one sheet next to the other, slightly overlapping, and tape it down on the edges so that it will be as flat as possible. Also, we ask the model to wipe her feet before tiptoeing into position.

The Mylar should really be handled with cotton gloves because it shows every mark. I noticed a wonderful phenomenon when, quite by accident, I turned the light straight down, directing it onto the Mylar surface. It bounced cloudlike patterns against the back wall and the finished picture had the appearance of an outdoor, beach background.

COMBINING IMAGES

Double exposures sometimes occur when we don't want them but with today's sophisticated cameras this is becoming less of a problem. There are, however, good uses for two pictures being combined into one. It is a popular practice in wedding photography and is used extensively in commercial ads.

There are three ways to do this: (1) on the film, (2) in the darkroom, or (3) by sandwiching two negatives or transparencies together.

DOUBLE EXPOSURE ON FILM

For complete separation of two images in the same picture, to make them look as though they were taken at one time, a black background is recommended. It is possible, of course, to combine two images (as happens in mistakes) with lighter backgrounds, but the first image will always be washed out by the second, thus the end result is never under control.

Let me run through the procedure that produced a model draped in an American flag, with fireworks to one side of the picture.

In my refrigerator I had saved a group of 4 x 5 color transparencies exposed three years earlier at a Fourth of July celebration but never developed. I had developed only one, at the time, just to make sure there were images on the film, but I had no idea whether or not the balance would still be good after so much time had elapsed.

I loaded one Grafmatic holder with these already exposed transparencies and loaded another with new, unexposed color. (Just in case the others were not good, I planned to shoot new fireworks.)

Using my 4 x 5 Gowlandflex camera, I placed my model against a black background in the studio with a #2 light (45 degrees front) and two #4s

167

Using an electric fan placed below model Stephanie McLean, fortunate that she was able to keep from blinking, we blew her hair away from both sides of her face. The front light is in the #1 position behind the camera, but the three backlights, one above her and two at #4 positions, create a white halo effect. Hasselblad with 150mm lens; slight retouching on negative.

What makes this star filter work is the sun hitting the water behind the model. Star filters need either a light shining into the lens or a reflection to produce the full effect. The filter used here is a Kordel 8-point star, which creates a triple image. High angle gives a clear background of shallow water. Hasselblad with 80mm lens. The sun was at the #5 position, directly above and behind model. Key light is in #1 position on the camera. *Model, Kerry Fotre.*

(45 degrees back), one from either side. I placed red cellophane over the two backlights. First I exposed a sheet of 4 x 5 Polaroid 559 film to establish the correct exposure and confirm the placement of the subject for when I made the new fireworks exposures.

I shot the first six sheets, varying only slightly the angle of the model's face, but making sure she remained in the same general area. Then I exposed the six new sheets of film. The first six were developed at the lab and I noted that, while the placement was good, the stillness of the air at the time the fireworks were exposed had caused a great deal of smoke in the background, taking away from the crisp effect that I wanted. Later, I photographed the fireworks with the second group of transparencies, making sure to keep them to one side. When these six were developed I was extremely pleased with the results.

So, in brief, when using black backgrounds, make sure to take a Polaroid shot for reference, or draw the image on the groundglass so that when you make your second exposure it will be in the right place. I've used this system when placing fire in the lower part of the picture. The fire was built in my fireplace and a black cloth covered the bricks so that only the fire was reproduced on the film.

It doesn't matter which image is exposed first. If you do not have a 4 x 5 camera it is possible to do this with some other cameras, but not all. The Hasselblad (2¼ x 2¼ format) with its removable back, enables the photographer to take a picture, replace the slide, remove the back, *then* turn the advance knob. Since the film has been removed, the same frame will be in place when the back is reinstated. I believe the Rolleiflex also comes with a mechanism for double exposures.

With 35mm cameras the end result is a bit more difficult to achieve. One method: When first loading the camera, take a marking pen and before closing the back, draw the rectangle of the frame on the film. Then, after running the film through the camera, rewind it, holding the camera up to your ear, carefully listening for a click as the film disconnects from the take-up spool. Stop winding immediately so that the film does not disappear into the cassette and you will have a piece of leader to start over again. Line up the leader with the frame that you have previously marked, making sure it is in alignment at a point where the take-up reel stops. It may take a couple of tries to get it exact. Then make your double exposures—they should come out at the right place!

A black background with a single strobe in a #3 position camera right can be used to make multiple exposures, as shown here. This can be done by firing a regular flash unit several times or by using a special stroboscopic electronic flash unit as used here, which can be set to fire as many times per second as the number of images desired, all done with one pass-through of action. However, with a conventional flash, which takes anywhere from 3 to 10 seconds to recycle, the model has to advance to the next position between flashes. Hasselblad with 80mm lens. *Model, Iris Rounsaville.*

MULTIPLE IMAGES ON BLACK

For this effect the subject must be lighted from the side, in a completely blackened room, against a black background. There is a special stroboscopic light on the market that can be rented for this purpose, but in lieu of using that strobe one can achieve the same thing with an ordinary electronic flash unit. The unit is not connected to your camera but is fired independently. Have the model rehearse in advance her movement across the film, always in profile, then set your camera on "bulb." Fire the flash with one hand (or have an assistant do it), holding the shutter open by using a cable release. The shutter remains open during the entire series of movements.

The reverse of this idea would be to have the model stand still and have something, such as a single light bulb, a fluorescent tube, or a sparkler, move across the background making a colorful pattern behind her. These are the same conditions that exist for the multiple exposures: a blackened room (or it could be outside at night in a darkened area), a camera on "bulb," and a flash unit fired independent of the shutter.

First you make a Polaroid test of the model alone, to arrive at the exposure for your single flash, this time from the front (#1) position, and a second Polaroid shot of the background activity. You are able to look at the two pictures and decide which f/stop and time of exposure is best to reproduce the light pattern and at what distance the flash should be to balance with that exposure.

Now pose the model in a pleasing composition (by using any type flood or modeling light if there is one on your flash unit). Turn all lights off and instruct the model to hold perfectly still while either you or an assistant moves whatever medium you have decided upon behind her. Since she is not lighted, only the pattern of those lights will be picked up on the film. The shutter is held open by bulb, as in the multiple-exposure picture. The lights may require one or two seconds but you will have arrived at that setting by using your Polaroid. Now, with the model remaining stationary, fire the flash. The results can be quite spectacular. It will no doubt be necessary to make several tries on various film frames in order to make sure the model did not move—and that the pattern is one you like.

DOUBLE EXPOSURE IN THE DARKROOM

Unlike working with the camera, where black is required for your second image, printed double images require white areas on which you will double-expose a second negative. The two negatives can be taken separately or you may already have two in your files that would do. An example is a photograph of a nude model, lying on Mylar in my studio. Her irregular reflection occupied the bottom portion of the frame and the balance was white. In my file I had a "special" cloud negative. I term it "special" because it was a comparatively small, round cloud with a very white center and stood out against a blue sky. I remember darkening the sky by using a yellow filter when I took the picture. The formation of the cloud was in a similar configuration to the model's pose and she fit perfectly into the white center area.

The darkroom procedure was to make four prints of the model, after having made a "test" strip to determine the correct exposure. These prints were marked on the back with the negative number, grade of paper, f/stop of enlarger, and number of seconds it took to print. Like this: 55/3/11/5. I was careful to do this penciling *after* I had made the exposure, otherwise the pencil marks would have come through on the print. Now I could make other prints without testing because I had this data. I was also careful to mark a small *x* at the top of the paper so that when it was replaced for the second exposure it would be in the correct position.

These prints were not developed but put in a lightproof box. Before removing the first negative, I marked the image on a piece of paper placed on the easel so that the cloud negative could be situated in the proper area.

I put the cloud negative in the enlarger, made a "test" strip to arrive at the correct exposure, then placed one of the previously exposed pieces of paper on the easel and printed the cloud over it.

After looking at the first result I decided to do some "dodging" and "burning." With a small piece of cardboard attached to a wire, I held back the center portion of the picture on the second print and burned in the corners to make them look darker. When dodging or burning, it is important to move the hand so that no sharp line of demarcation is shown between the darker or lighter areas. The picture was successful mainly because the cloud had that light area in the middle. Had it been dark it would have printed over my model.

THE OLD SANDWICH TRICK

I have never tried sandwiching black-and-white negatives but I've done it successfully with color slides. I imagine it could be done with black and white as well; that might be an interesting project to be tackled at a later date. When combining slides I generally intend to project them, as I do when giving a seminar or lecture. I've found that it helps if the two transparencies are slightly overexposed so that their combined densities create a normal appearance.

THE PICTURE-IN-A-PICTURE TRICK

This is almost too easy. Make a print of a girl, mount or paste it on cardboard, and cut it out. It could be color or black and white. Then decide where you want this girl to be—in a field, or in a bowl of cherries—and place the cardboard image at whichever situation you've selected. Now take another photo of that picture within a picture. It's amazing how realistic it can be. Recently I was given a spectacular black-and-white print by the accomplished photographer Newton, who has exhibited in many photographic art galleries throughout the country. The picture was taken in Alaska and is called "Horse" because near the corner of this magnificent expanse of Alaskan glacier and field is the silhouette of one lone horse, looking so tiny that you hardly see him at first glance. When I noted this, I laughingly suggested to Newton that he make up a series of cardboard animals and carry them along when he goes on his hikes for panoramic views so that at the last minute he can stick the figure in the foreground. Newton didn't think it was funny, which I can understand because he, like Edward Weston and Ansel Adams before him, is a purist and would never resort to tricks like I do.

I still think the idea has merit, especially for me, because I could make my cardboards from nude figures already on file and thus have no problem with the law when trying to photograph outdoors in areas where nudity is forbidden.

BLURRED BACKGROUND OUTDOORS

Creating a blurred background outdoors is similar in a way to the night shot where the lights moved behind the model. But we are working with daylight and an interesting background might be difficult to find. The results can be fun if you have objects move behind her, such as cars, cyclists, or people, blurred by slow shutter speeds.

Set your camera on a tripod and pose your model so that she does not move, because your shutter speeds will be $\frac{1}{8}$, $\frac{1}{15}$, $\frac{1}{30}$ second. In a shot with cars, I was able to situate my model at the edge of the street and, using my 200mm lens, line her up in a position that was pleasing. Then I watched the traffic, not through the finder, but with my naked eye, and just before the car intersected the image of her body, I snapped the shutter. The cars stretched out across the whole background.

FRONT PROJECTION

Front projection is not for the aspiring photographer who takes pictures only once in a while. This costly equipment is used mainly by large commercial or portrait studios that wish to place their subjects in faraway places or whose geographic location limits their accessibility to outdoor backgrounds.

This system is based on two principles: (1) the 45-degree partial-reflection mirror (beam-splitter) and (2) the lenticular screen, which reflects light better than any other surface. The camera is set up with the mirror at 45 degrees in front of the lens. A strobe light projects a scenic slide up to the mirror, which reflects the image onto the model and the screen background. Both images, that of the model and the slide, are reflected back to the camera, through the mirror, to the lens.

Even though the scene of the slide is projected over the model's body, the scene is not picked up in the camera's eye. The image on the flesh is very faint so that the main light washes it out. However, the screen, because of its special design (extremely reflective surface), picks up the scene. In the final result, the subject appears to be in an outdoor setting (or whatever subject was selected for the slide).

There are drawbacks to this system. First, the model must stand no farther than 4 feet from the background. She must be lighted from the side and those lights must have louvers or baffles to prevent light from hitting the background screen. Also, both the lens of the camera and the lens of the projector must be in perfect alignment.

Using Mylar to capture reflections in a daylight studio, with one 600-watt quartz spot aimed down at the Mylar from a #3 position, resulted in a cloudlike effect on the background. Ambient light from the studio window at camera right lighted the model's face and gave a bit more light to the body. Background is curved plaster wall with no seam. Hasselblad with 80mm lens. *Model, Sara Munson.*

In a conventional room setting Mylar was used on the floor but the seam shows where the wall intersects the floor. Background is lighted by two lights and the model has one light on her from the front, in the #1 position, with a Larson 36-inch Soff Box and Norman 800-watt-second power pack into which all three lights were plugged. Hasselblad with 80mm lens. *Model, Lesley Heasler.*

Mylar was used on the curved studio floor with no light on the model and four lights, Larson Strobosols, directed to the background. Enough light spilled onto the body to give the effect of two lights in the #4 positions, three-quarter rear. Exposure was based more on the highlights than the shadows because we wanted the body to appear dark. Mylar comes only in 54-inch widths, so it is hard to avoid a seam when two sheets are used. *Model, Shawna Roebuck.*

Same negative was used in both pictures. Combining cloud negative with nude on plain background (described in text) is a darkroom technique that can add another dimension to a picture. The cloud negative required only 25 percent of the printing time of the first negative. Two different cloud negatives were used. The first showed trees that look like bushes in the foreground, and the second was a cloud only. *Model, Shawna Roebuck.*

Model Bettina brought her pet snake with her for our sitting, and we worked on a wet terrazzo floor to get reflections. The seamless plaster curve in the studio eliminates any line to the background. Lighting was four Strobosols on the background, which reflected light onto the body.

I had a choice of where to put the horizon in printing this double negative and figured the only logical place was to locate it at the same camera elevation as the original picture. In noting that one looks up at her head but down at her feet, it was obvious that the horizon had to be at midpoint. The main difficulty in printing this was trying to eliminate the line going through her waist. I burned in that area separately by using a small hole in a piece of cardboard. *Model, Bettina.*

Original picture with no texture screen. Taken with a light in the #3 position on the left and lights on the background from the right. These were quartz lights. Pentax with 55mm lens. *Model, Kori Kody.*

Using a grain texture screen placed about 1/4 inch above the paper during printing, I first exposed the negative without the screen and then gave it the same amount of exposure with the screen in place. *Model, Kori Kody.*

Etching screen placed in contact with the paper and exposed for total exposure. *Model, Kori Kody.*

Etching screen placed approximately 1/4 inch above paper. Picture was exposed first, then screen was given the same amount. Picture received 100 percent, screen 50 percent. *Model, Kori Kody.*

Rubenesque figure model in sylvan setting is an excellent subject for grain screen since screen gives the effect of a painting or a drawing. The stairway in first picture was in the shade; tub in second was in the sun. Both pictures taken with Pentax, using 50mm macro lens. *Model, Carolyne Singer.*

This picture was created by combining the negative of the model with a negative of a tree. The tree was printed first with the enlarger set at f/8 for 5 seconds. The model was printed with the enlarger set at f/16 for 7 seconds. These exposures were determined by making a test strip first and making a note on the back of the print. After selecting a tree, I purposely shot it on an overcast day to get a background of white sky. Hasselblad with 150mm lens for the tree and 80mm lens for the model. *Model, Lesley Heasler.*

A good example of "the angle of reflection is equal to the angle of incidence."
In other words, why does the star filter reflect from only one shoulder? Because
the light was coming directly down upon her shoulder and bouncing into the
lens. Kordel 8-point star filter. The key light was at the #2 position from the left,
and the fill was a small strobe from the #1 position, next to camera. Two
backlights were at the #4 position to highlight the figure and hair. The hair
boom from above was the light that created the star filter. *Model, Yvonne
Thomas.*

This complicated setup is the result of eight pictures! We built this set of tile with wading pool in our driveway, with Summitville Tile Co. laying the tile. The picture was taken with a Gowland-flex 4 x 5 camera, shooting down from a ladder. The sun was coming from camera right in the #4 position; a reflector was used in the #4 position camera left. A Norman 200-B strobe was used at the #2 position camera left. The six floating tiles were taken in individual shots and later put in by the art department. A second 4 x 5 color transparency was taken of two models at the beach, a windsurfer and a

female model. Later, the two transparencies were combined with those of the tiles and additional artwork, which included placing the company logo (the sun) on the horizon and on the sail. The logo was already printed on the T-shirt. The finished picture is far too busy for my taste but very cleverly put together. I feel that the picture would have been improved with the windsurfer taking the spot of the girl in the background and eliminating her as well as the sun and the extra tiles. *Foreground model, Nancy Fletcher; running model, Stephanie McLean.*

Window light can create moodiness, so by combining this with a sexy body and a pretty face we have an excellent setting for a calendar picture. Here, the direct sun, coming in at a #4 position, was almost too bright, causing the loss of some detail on the leg and chest; however, this was balanced out by the overall effect. The only additional lighting used were the two 17-inch translucents in a vertical configuration at the #2 position. In retrospect, the harsh sun could have been softened by hanging a white sheet outside the building to filter the sunlight. *Model, Catherine Lansing.*

11

SYNCHRO-SUN
SIMPLIFIED

The term "synchro-sun" refers to the use of electronic flash outdoors with sunlight. There are two questions I am asked about this system: Why do you use strobe on the beach? and How does one calculate strobe with sunlight? I find that even many professional photographers still have trouble understanding and conquering the mathematics of this combination of light and thus avoid using it, preferring instead to employ the use of reflectors.

Any photographer who looks at my outdoor pictures realizes that the majority of them are taken with the combination of sunlight and flash. The brighter the sun, the more I depend on strobe to "modify" its unflattering shadows. During the peak hours of the day the sun is in the wrong place for glamour photography—high in the sky. It is those early morning and late afternoon hours that provide a low angle of rays. Remember how I emphasize the bad effect of "top" light? Well, the sun at midday is just that.

The major problem is finding models who will get up early enough to be on location at these hours. Of course, when I work with agency girls they'll be on time, but the fee is time-and-a-half for hours before 8 A.M. and after 6 P.M.

You'll note that I continually refer to beach locations but the same lighting conditions of sun and strobe apply to any outdoor setting.

But why don't you use a silver reflector? you might ask. My answer is that looking into a reflector is like looking into the sun itself. It is impossible to avoid squinting. I do use a reflector as an additional "kick" light (it becomes a second sun) to the side, much as I do in the studio with strobe lights. This illumination to the edge of the body gives an added brilliance to the photograph. I refer to this as my 1-4-4 lighting. The #1 position uses the strobe from the front and the first #4 refers to the sun; the second #4 uses the reflector. (All of these placements according to number are discussed in chapter 1.)

Now, getting to the important, and usually most confusing, area—the system for balancing the intensity of the strobe with the intensity of the sun. First, remember that when I use strobe outdoors, I use it the same way as when I'm in the studio. The strobe is what determines the skin tones and correct exposure *on the model.* The strobe is controlled both by the f/stop and the distance at which it is placed from the subject. It will have no effect on the background because it is limited in the extent to which it carries forward. I've seen young people at rock concerts, way back in the theater, shoot off a flash toward the stage. It will do absolutely nothing!

We want to use our shutter speed to control how much light (from the sun) is allowed to be exposed onto the film for the background and the f/stop and distance to control the amount of light on the model. Memorize that.

There is no way you are going to do this successfully if you do not make a test with your particular camera, strobe, and film to determine the amount of light output at the varying distances. So I suggest the following procedure:

1. Select your favorite location with sun behind the model. It is not necessary to have sun on her face.
2. Load your camera with your favorite film. I use ASA 100 transparency with my 2¼ x 2¼ Hasselblad.
3. Place your camera on a tripod.
4. Attach your strobe unit to a stand, 10 feet from your subject. Measure this with a tape. It is important to know the exact distance.
5. Make sure the strobe head is directed at the model and is close to the angle from which the camera is stationed. The camera may move in closer to the subject or back away, but the strobe remains at 10 feet.
6. As a starting point set your shutter speed according to directions on the paper inside the film box. Usually a speed of 1/125 second is a good beginning.
7. Most electronic flash manufacturers suggest a "guide number" for their unit with film ASA numbers. For example, if 80 is the indicated number for the film speed you are using, divide the distance of the strobe (10 feet) into 80 and you get 8. You

would set your diaphragm at f/8. If there is no guide number, then there should be a dial chart attached that will give you the estimated f/stops for the varying distances. So, set your f/stop.

8. Make your first exposure at, say, f/8 and then run the gamut to see just what the light will do at the various f/stops.

9. Develop the film and make a note or chart that indicates the most favorable f/stop according to the results.

With my equipment I have made this test and find that f/9.5 (between f/8 and f/11) works at 10 feet. I've taped that to my strobe for easy reference and all other distances are calculated from that point.

You'll notice we did not mention the background. That's because I want you to concentrate only on what the strobe is doing. The background will be controlled, as mentioned before, by the shutter speed.

I have found that a large range of shutter speeds apply to the control of background exposure. The exact setting will depend on the amount of reflection present. For example, when shooting in the surf I may use 1/400 second to cut down the amount of exposure to the white foam. In the woods I go as slow as 1/30 second to allow as much light as possible to brighten the foliage (green, incidentally, requires about twice the exposure of any other color). In these extreme conditions I may change the f/stop as well. For instance, with my Norman 200-B and the white foam of the surf I go from the normal f/9.5 to f/11 because the model also is getting a dose of reflection from the foam. In the woods I may open up one-half stop to f/8 because of the absorption quality of the green.

Not all of the foregoing may be of help to those who have cameras that do not sync at fast shutter speeds. Some 35mm models, with focal plane shutters, cannot sync faster than 1/60 or 1/100, so they are unable to control excessive background light such as that at the beach or in the desert or that of snow. However, the system works okay where the background exposures would range from 1/60 to 1/100.

Here comes the hard part: The system is easy if the strobe remains at 10 feet. I can move in and out with my camera, but most of the time when I work outdoors I put the strobe *on* my camera. I like it to come directly from the same direction as the lens. If this is the case, and I want to move closer I will have to change both the f/stop and the shutter speed accordingly. The f/stop is changed to control the strobe which is now closer and thus will overexpose my subject. The smaller f/stop cuts down the exposure on the background so that I must give a longer amount of time by increasing the shutter speed as well. Divide the guide number by the distance of the strobe: 80 ÷ 6 feet = 13.5, or f/13 (between f/11 and f/16). That's about a stop and a half. The shutter speed must be decreased by the same amount, say, from 1/250 to 1/125.

The same scene with and without the electronic flash. Here, one might think the white foam would be enough to illuminate the backlighted body of model Shelly Winnaman, but without the flash we see no details in the face or bosom area. The picture is improved 100 percent with the addition of the Norman 200-B strobe to the camera and measured to the correct distance so that it balances out the background. Hasselblad with 80mm lens. Sun was at the #4 position.

The wonderful part about working with the Hasselblad is that the shutter speed and f/stops can be locked so that when you change the setting in either direction the shutter speed automatically changes with it.

Nevertheless, when photographing a beautiful girl one doesn't want to stop and calibrate, so a chart typed on a card and attached to the strobe will avoid delays. I also have my assistant control the strobe; he moves in

and out or stays put, as directed. This arrangement is much easier than working with a stand in sand or surf. The following is a chart that I have attached to my strobe unit:

	Woods	Lawn	Pool	Beach	Foam
10-foot Norman 200-B	1/30	1/60	1/125	1/250	1/400
Film ASA 100	f/8	f/8	f/8	f/9	f/11

I highly recommend that you make such a test with your electronic flash unit in relation to film and background. The chart above can be used as a starting point. The reflective situations could apply to almost any situation. When you test equipment you might find that you have a smaller guide number. It might be 60 or 40 or even 20. You can make your chart accordingly.

These four pictures were taken with the Norman 200-B electronic flash on the camera with the sun in back of each model at the #5 position. Camera was the Hasselblad with 80mm lens. In each instance, a Polaroid test was made on the Gowlandflex 4 x 5, so we were careful to match the conditions of the finished picture with that of the Polaroid—with the foam either in or out. Otherwise, the end results could have been either under- or overexposed. Sometimes, for effect, I purposely overexpose the background by using a slower shutter speed, as in the picture below, left. *Models, Caroline Stone (first picture), Nancy Fletcher (second picture), Debbie Shelton (third and fourth).*

When working in gardens I am careful to find areas where the sun can backlight my model and create the black areas that will cause her to stand out. Here, the model is placed so that the sun is in the #5 position, directly behind her, with her hair receiving light at the top and on both sides. The flash is in the #1 position on the camera, giving her the beneficial front light. Although the green foliage is flattering to the model in the color photograph, the black-and-white prints are overly busy, but this is my personal taste. Hasselblad with 80mm lens; Norman 200-B strobe on camera in #1 position. *Model, Caroline Bartlett.*

These two pictures employ the same techniques shown in the three photographs on page 193. *Models, Kerry Fotre (first picture) and Caroline Stone.*

An outdoor portrait enhanced by the black background. With the 150mm lens on the Hasselblad and the sun coming from the #4 position camera left, the Norman 200-B strobe takes the #2 position camera right. *Model, Marina Moore.*

With sunlight coming through a window, shadows can be very harsh for the model but good for bringing out the texture in clothing. To soften the shadows I used two 17-inch Larson translucent umbrellas mounted on an aluminum bar with two Norman strobe heads plugged into a 200-B power pack by means of a Y-cable. Though this is the same lighting bar that I use horizontally for portraits, I have in this case placed it in the vertical position with the camera in between the two translucents. *Model, Amie Johnson.*

With the sun as the only light source, in the first picture we lose part of the body to shadows even though the texture of the garment is exaggerated. The shadows are softened by using the Norman 200-B heads through two translucents. Model was also moved away from the wall slightly so that light hits the background. The sun was coming from the #3 position and the fill-in light was at the #2 position. Hasselblad with 80mm lens. *Model, Shelly Winnaman.*

Posing in a window setting with strong sun coming through from a #5 position causes highlights, which can be emphasized by using diffusion filters. Hasselblad with 80mm lens and a Harrison & Harrison #3 filter over the lens. Two Larson 17-inch translucents were attached vertically to a bar and placed at side of camera. *Model, Shawna Roebuck.*

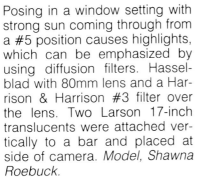

The sun is directly behind model with the flash in #1 position on the camera. Clear water from a spring, cascading over a rock on its way to the ocean, lent a bit of action to the picture. Hasselblad with Norman 200-B electronic flash. *Model, Caroline Stone.*

In most cases I have the sunlight behind the model and use the electronic flash as a key light in the #1 position. Here, the sun is in a #2 position from the right side and the flash is on the camera, filling in the shadows slightly. Hasselblad with 80mm lens and Norman 200-B strobe. *Model, Anita Bradford.*

←
Working in the confined area of a small bathroom that had a skylight presented special problems. The translucents reflected in the glass behind the model, so we switched to one Norman head. By watching the glass when we fired the Norman we could see where it should be placed. Some of it can be seen in the final result, but it is mixed in with the foliage and doesn't distract from the model. Hasselblad was used for black and white, Gowlandflex 4 x 5 for color transparencies. *Model, Iris Condon.*

199

Calendar markets and novelty companies purchase nude subjects such as this picture, where the model is pretty of face and figure, looks directly into the camera, and is usually in a bedroom setting. Lighting was a Larson Starfish in the #2 position camera right, with a second light placed on the bed and directed toward the background. Color was shot with 4 x 5 Gowlandflex. These markets rarely purchase black and white. *Model, Alexandra Day.*

12

MAKING MONEY WITH
YOUR PHOTOGRAPHS

You've found a pretty girl and want to try out your new 35mm camera, maybe make a little money on the side by selling the pictures. If this is the case, you'll need to pay attention to details that would otherwise not enter into the activity if the purpose were only to improve your own glamour techniques.

Of primary concern is the model herself. It's one thing to have a pretty girlfriend, but editors and ad agency executives don't have the benefit of your personal contact. They judge solely by how the young woman comes across in the pictures. What may look attractive to you may not appeal to them. Keep in mind that these people are bombarded with photographs from professional modeling agencies; they're used to seeing beauty at its best.

Always begin with the face. Facial features can be embellished with makeup but the basic structure cannot be changed. If a girl has a long jaw, a long nose, eyes close together, unattractive teeth, these will not be changed with cosmetics. Try for as much symmetry as possible in the features. Just a millimeter too much or too little will lower the chances of a girl's being accepted by those who make the final selection in the field of glamour.

When I've made these comments to photographers who are having difficulty selling their pictures, they invariably make such statements as, "Well, I don't think Brooke Shields is so pretty." What such an observation tells me is that that person is letting his personal preference interfere with his ability to "see" what the advertisers consider to be a moneymaking attraction.

The entire selection of models in an agency's file will probably not stand up to the tough kind of scrutiny I'm talking about. That's because there are many jobs for which the client needs a group of ten or more girls, all photographed at full-length, at a distance, in a variety of clothing styles. Here, the facial features, while important, are not as meticulously dissected. As long as the girl is well groomed, can pose, is graceful, and has an overall flare for bringing life to the photographs, that's what counts.

In my own work, my clients are looking at the girl *only*. Not the clothing. Even the product becomes secondary. This is the kind of model who falls into the category of "stock" photographs that can be sold to a number of advertisers for different products—to calendar companies, to travel groups for brochures, and so on.

Because I have, during my career as a photographer, focused on the California Girl look—the young, wholesome beauty romping in the southern California surf—I am contacted by a variety of clients, all wanting to see what I have on file with that look. I've broadened the inventory in recent years by including other sporty costumes such as shorts, jeans, and even dresses to accommodate the more conservative advertisers. But I have tried to stick to my original conviction that the face comes first, and have had this confirmed by high sales of those models whom I've selected with great scrutiny and rejection of those where I have compromised, thinking my photography would magically correct any doubts that I had.

So, rule number one: Select a girl with a youthful complexion, large eyes, small nose, beautiful smile, healthy hair.

Her figure is important also, but one can make some corrections here, with angle and pose. It is still preferable not to have the worry of making such adjustments, but if you've found a girl with a gorgeous face and a mediocre figure, it is possible to make the combination work. However, a gorgeous figure and a mediocre face is not as easy to sell.

Finding subjects with the demanding qualities described is no easy task and doesn't happen every day. Also, when a girl says she's with a modeling agency, that does not guarantee that she qualifies for stock photographs. Some agencies and modeling schools are more interested in making money from enrollment of students than from collecting the percentage they would get from the students' modeling jobs, so they are not as selective. Top agencies do not take *everyone* who comes along— and they do not charge a fee, only take a commission when they have obtained a job for the model.

Always interview a girl in person; do not depend on photographs that you have seen. Changes take place—maybe she has lost or gained weight, cut or bleached her hair.

Calendar companies want pictures shot horizontally with the possibility of cropping to vertical, which gives them double use of each picture. Lighting was a bank of four 36-inch translucents, two on either side of the camera. A boom light was used for the model's hair and spilled onto her shoulder. Hasselblad was used for the black and white and the Gowlandflex 4 x 5 for color. *Model, Linda Johnson.*

Seasonal ideas, such as Valentine's Day, Christmas, Halloween, are always good for stock files. This picture was taken in 4 x 5 color transparency with the 4 x 5 Gowlandflex using a 210mm lens, with Ektachrome ASA 64 film. A 72-inch Larson Hex on the Gowland Swing Light was placed at the #2 position camera right, with a hair light and four background lights. The black and white was made with the Hasselblad and 80mm lens. *Model, Audrey Bradshaw.*

What about payment? If we use someone from an agency on an assignment, we pay the going hourly rate for that person or we make an agreement for a flat rate *before* the shooting. If we are doing a speculative shooting, photographs for our color file, we generally cannot use an agency model. They want to know where every picture is going and to be paid for every sale. Since that cannot be guaranteed, we do not have access to those girls. However, we do run into models who need photographs. If they meet our standards, we make an agreement to pay them a flat fee of a previously agreed-upon amount, plus pictures. The fee is naturally less than they would get if they were with an agency. But, they are receiving an excellent portfolio, worth even more than their hourly rate. Sometimes we do an exchange where we give just photographs, no money (except for that $1.00 mentioned in the model release) in exchange for the release. The reason for the lower payment on stock photographs is that they do not command as high a rate of payment from the advertisers and we depend on multiple sale of the same picture in order to get our investment back. I've found that working with girls who have a professional attitude has always resulted in a good relationship and no question about the future sales. Sometimes we have used subjects who have never posed before, but who feel a certain skepticism and worry that we will be making thousands of dollars on their photographs. I wish that this were so. But, again, stock photographs always sell for a fraction of what an assignment would pay.

Another method of payment is to give an agreed-upon percentage of sales, say, from 10 to 25 percent. The problem with this is that pictures don't always sell immediately, sometimes not for two or three years. So the burden of keeping track of all sales and knowing how to reach the subject falls on the photographer. The model may have moved in the meantime and could, at a later date, come back and say she was not paid, forgetting that she did not let anyone know where she was!

If you have limited funds and no access to markets, it is wise to seek out a stock photo agency to sell your pictures. With this method you get only 40 to 50 percent of the sale and the agency takes the rest. But consider the effort they go to—contacting clients, sending out the pictures over and over again, keeping accurate records. They will want you to produce—send material to them on a regular basis. They're not interested in handling someone who takes pictures only occasionally. *All pictures must have releases*.

The following books list the major stock agents in the United States and would be worth having:

Photography Market Place. R. R. Bowker, 1180 Avenue of the Americas, New York, NY 10036.

Photographer's Market. Writer's Digest Books, 9933 Alliance Road, Cincinnati, OH 45242.

Another book that I recommend if you wish to *sell* your pictures is:

Selling Your Photography. Arie Kopelman and Tad Crawford, St. Martin's Press, 175 Fifth Avenue, New York NY 10010.

This book will give you all the legal information that is necessary and so important to the business of selling photographs.

The following is a list of calendar companies that purchase glamour subjects:

U. O. Colson
Paris, IL 61944

Osborn-Kemper-Thomas
Calendar Hill
Cincinnati, OH 45204

Skinner Kennedy
9451 Natural Bridge Road
St. Louis, MO 63134

McCleery-Cumming Company
915 East Tyler
Washington, IA 52353

Parktone Press
P.O. Box 539
Spring Valley, NY 10977

Kaeser and Blair, Inc.
953 Martin Place
Cincinnati, OH 45202

Shaw Barton
Coshocton, OH 43812

Brown and Bigelow
345 Plato Boulevard East
St. Paul, MN 55107

John Baumgarth Company
3001 North Avenue
Melrose Park, IL 60160

Write to these people and inquire about their needs, asking what size transparency they require, what subject matter, what their schedule of payment is. Most, if not all, will be happy to give you this information.

Your photographs, preferably transparencies for selling, must be of the highest quality. No overexposure, underexposure, out of focus, or bad backgrounds accepted. These markets are used to dealing with professionals who send in only technically perfect transparencies.

The best bit of advice we can give you is to learn to be technically accurate before thinking of selling. Study the various markets. Advertisers tend to stick with a particular style and subject, so this will give you a clue as to your background, clothing, props. Be particular when selecting a model for salable material. Then, take lots of pictures—and send them out!

Another idea for stock photos is to combine glamour with money or the suggestion of money. This picture is better as a black and white and has been used in several trade journals. Lighting was from the #1 position, using the Larson 72-inch Reflectasol on the Gowland Swing Light and one light on background. Hasselblad with 80mm lens. *Model, Shelly Winnaman.*

Although model Lisa Auld looks like "the girl next door," she is actually prettier and that is what makes her a good subject for stock photos that can be sold for all types of ads. The horizontal composition and white area make it possible for advertisers to insert copy about their product. The Gowland Swing Light from a #2 position camera right adds roundness to model's figure. A trick to remember is that the forward shoulder should always point to the direction of the light to get cross light, which emphasizes cleavage. Four smaller strobes were used directly on the background.

With health clubs and exercise being so popular today, stock photographs that show a pretty girl in exercise clothes are in demand. Extremely flat lighting was achieved by using the Gowland Swing Light in a #2 position camera right and two 36-inch Larson Reflectasols camera left from the #1 position. Two lights on background washed out any possible shadows. Hasselblad with 80mm lens. *Model, Rhenette Watkins.*

Unusual contortions of a pretty girl lend themselves to the stock photo market. Advertisers are always looking for a gimmick, as in this case, where the model points as if to say, "He went thataway." Believe it or not, this model works in a mortuary at night. Gowland Swing Light in a #2 position camera left with two lights on the background on the right side. Hasselblad with 80mm lens. *Model, Margaret Shumar.*

Once in a while we find a model with special talents, such as Aleta Ashley, who is also a mime and applies her own makeup. Pictures like these are great for a stock file. Lighting was the Gowland Swing Light with the 72-inch Larson Hex and Norman 2000-watt-second strobe from the #1 position behind the camera. Two Strobosols were on the background. Hasselblad with 80mm lens and 150mm lens for close-up.

A pretty girl with a great figure posing by side of pool with colorful flowers nearby is a typical calendar and stock photo subject. Sun is directly behind the model, lighting her hair from a #5 position. The key light, a Norman 200-B strobe, is attached to the camera in the #1 position. Black and white was taken with Hasselblad and 80mm lens. Color was taken of same setup with 4 x 5 Gowlandflex and 180mm Rodenstock Sironar lens. When working around a swimming pool you usually have to shoot down to gain a clear background. A rule of thumb is that when the model is in a kneeling position the camera is placed at her eye level. *Model, Holly Huddleston.*

Believe it or not, this is a wet suit—one of those rubber things worn to keep swimmers warm in winter! At any rate, model Shelly Winnaman makes it look good. This picture was taken for the Fuji film company to test their 4 x 5 Fujichrome ASA 50 and ASA 100 with various filters. Black and white was taken with the Hasselblad, using the 80mm lens. Color was taken with the Gowlandflex and 180mm lens.

Normally I would shoot a model from waist level but in this case the background was not attractive, and in order to bring the horse's head close to the model against a clear area, the camera had to be higher than usual. A pretty girl with a horse is always a popular subject with calendar companies. Black and white was taken with the Hasselblad and 80mm lens. Color was taken with Gowlandflex 4 x 5. One light, a Norman 200-B head, was held by an assistant in a #2 position, aimed at the horse, which was so much darker than the model. The other Norman head was on the camera in the #1 position. A Y-cable connected the two to the power pack. Sunlight was directly behind. *Model, Stephanie McLean.*

Aya is an artist whose hands are used for commercial ads because of their smooth skin and tapered fingers. Two #4 lights, one from either side at the back, and a 72-inch Larson Hex on the Gowland Swing Light at the #2 position camera right outline the beads and hands against a black background. Backlights are always overexposed because they are lighting only a small area (edge-light), which produces the white necessary to separate the subject from the background. Hasselblad with 150mm lens was used for both color and black and white. *Model, Aya Imai.*

Couples enjoying themselves with food, music, or sports are always good as subjects for stock photographs. Here, we set up a picnic on a patio and took a series of photographs at night. Lighting was tungsten. The key light was a #2 left, the hair light a #4 right, with one light on the ceiling in the background. *Models, Christopher Crawford and Cristen Kauffman.*

INDEX